T0115684

TAROT

SIMPLIFIED

TAROT
SIMPLIFIED

THE ESSENTIAL GUIDE TO THE BASICS

ISABELLA FERRARI

○
○
○

DEYST.

An Imprint of WILLIAM MORROW

CONTENTS

INTRODUCTION

✦ ✴ ✦

Tarot cards attract people for a variety of different reasons. You might be looking for answers regarding your personal life, in matters such as love, family, or money. Or you may be approaching witchcraft and the occult world, wanting to learn more about this mysterious and beautiful An practice.

Whether you're at a crossroads in your life or are simply curious about this topic, tarot cards will be your window to a magickal world where introspection and divination reign supreme. This practice will reveal hidden aspects of your life and much more; it will bring to light the answers to difficult questions and help you understand what the future will bring.

A tarot reading has the power to tell you the best decision to make, as well as what you should no longer pursue; it can show unseen lies and predict new love; it will help you understand what's inside your mind and heart; and it might sometimes give you answers that you won't like.

Your tarot deck will be your most sincere and truthful friend, a guide on which you can rely, and one that will accompany you on your spiritual journey.

As each card has its own meaning—which is a combination of a clear message and a matter of personal interpretation—learning to read the cards is not an easy skill to master.

Whether you'd like to become a tarot reader or just want to read the cards for yourself, knowledge and experience are a winning combination that will help you understand each card more and more. Your experience with your tarot deck will be the most powerful tool in your belt when it comes to doing an accurate reading.

When writing this book, I tried to create something that anyone who wants to approach the tarot world can use: a step-by-step guide that provides a little bit of history as well as the meaning of each card and how to use it in a magickal practice ("magick" with a k is distinct from "magic," which refers to the mundane tricks of magicians). This beautiful practice is so vast and so full of different details and interpretations that it is, in my opinion, impossible and almost inappropriate to attempt to write a strict guide that tells you exactly what to do and how to use the cards.

Instead, as you're reading this book, keep an open mind and always embrace your curiosity and intuition regarding signs and messages from your deck. Each of us will have a unique experience with our deck of tarot cards, which will be a practice in growth and mystery. And although these mysteries cannot be solved entirely, you can use this guide to get a little closer to the truth.

CHAPTER ONE

THE BASICS

A BRIEF HISTORY OF TAROT

The origins of tarot cards are still unknown, as there are many theories that attempt to explain where they were invented. Some say they were created by ancient priests in Egypt, and others believe they were created in Europe. Others suppose they could have come from the Middle East, or they could have been introduced by the Romani. The first recorded tarot deck was created in Italy in the 1440s. As printed cards didn't exist yet, each card was hand-painted, so they weren't cheap.

One of the earliest decks was composed of the Batons, Coins, Swords, and Cups, still used in many games in Italy, Spain, and Portugal and for modern divination practices. After that, additional trump cards were added to the deck, which were named *"carte da trionfi,"* triumph cards. These cards were initially used for entertainment—a game to play.

We can find the first rules in a book by Martiano da Tortona in the 15th century; the book describes that the first set of 60 cards included 44 birds and 16 Roman gods, who were the triumph cards. Although we can find many different representations that have been created since Tortona's time, the game's rules have remained the same to this day, with the occult practices originating in the 18th century.

It isn't until 1502 that we can find the use of the word *tarocho*, or "tarot," in modern Italian, *tarocco* for the singular use and *tarocchi* for the plural. While the origin of the word is uncertain, the term was also a synonym for "foolishness," and you can still use this word to indicate something fake.

Tarot cards were initially played as a game and we didn't see the implementation of cartomancy until the mid-1700s. Even though the first recorded proof of this practice was in 1750 with the deck "Tarocco Bolognese," the use of tarot cards became far more popular during the 1780s thanks to Etteila (the first person to issue a deck exclusively for occult purposes) and the deck "Tarot of Marseilles."

Etteila's deck was divided into two parts: Major Arcana and Minor Arcana. Major Arcana are 22 cards meant to hold the secrets of your spiritual life and human experiences. Minor Arcana are 56 cards intended to relate to what we experience in our everyday life.

Today, tarot cards are used for both purposes— to play, and to read the future and reveal hidden answers.

There are many ways to read and utilize the cards, mainly based in the practice of witchcraft, and we will dive into each of these in the following chapters.

THE DIFFERENT DECKS

Today, tarot cards have become more popular than ever. That's why you can find almost any type of tarot deck; the illustrations can feature different animals, movies, cartoons, and much more. The card's shape is typically rectangular, and it can vary in size. You can find oversized cards or you can pick a smaller deck, suitable for your bag or suitcase.

There are some exceptions regarding the shape and number of cards. For example, the Earthair Experimental Elemental Tarot are square, and you'll find 95 cards: 23 Major Arcana, 72 Minor Arcana, and 16 extra cards.

Many decks also come with a complimentary guide to help you understand the meaning of each tarot card and how to spread them.

Let's take a look at the main tarot decks you might find in the tarot world:

THE RIDER-WAITE-SMITH DECK:

Arthur Edward Waite was one of the most famous occultists of the 20th century. He commissioned Pamela Smith, a theatrical designer, to design his tarot deck in 1909, which is still the most popular today. Arthur and Pamela belonged to the Hermetic Order of the Golden Dawn, a famous mystical society where Edward was Grand Master. That is why the cards represent many symbols connected to the Golden Dawn.

Thanks to Pamela's work, with this deck, readers could understand the cards' meanings by looking at them, as each illustration told a story. The deck was first published in 1910, and since then many different variations have been sold. The exact artwork may be different, but what each card represents will remain consistent across all versions. The deck has continued evolving and changing to this day.

THE THOTH TAROT:

This famous deck was painted between 1938 and 1943 by Lady Frieda Harris, following the direction of Aleister Crowley, a well-known English occultist. It was published in 1969 after both Crowley and Harris had died. Crowley also wrote a book, *The Book of Thoth*, which was meant to be used with the deck.

The deck presents extravagant and colorful cards that encapsulate the spirit of the infamous Crowley. We can observe symbols related to astrology, philosophy, and science.

THE MARSEILLES DECK:

One of the oldest tarot decks, originating in the 1700s, this comes from the region of Marseille in France. The Marseilles Deck still has Minor and Major Arcana, but when you look at representation of the Minor you will only see numbered symbols without the "storytelling" elements we find in decks like the Rider-Waite-Smith. This is because the Marseilles Deck was originally meant to be a game to play.

The first such deck we know of was printed by Pierre Madenie of Dijon in 1709. In 1760, Nicolas Conver engraved them in his factory; by then it had become one of the most popular decks ever used.

HOW TO PREPARE FOR A READING

Asking ourselves what the future will bring is a practice that even our oldest ancestors engaged in. Since ancient times, throughout different eras and cultures, people have always wondered if it could be possible to predict fate. When using tarot, we have the chance to connect with our psychic abilities and seek answers and guidance regarding our life.

Although tarot readings with a professional can be much easier and no doubt very informative, it is also interesting to learn how to use this powerful tool ourselves.

It is important to find a deck that resonates with us. That often comes as a subtle feeling, a voice that tells us that that specific deck is the right one for us.

Once we have found our deck, it is important to be kind with ourselves and allow the slow process of learning to happen. Building strong connections with our deck will require time and patience as we grow our skills and knowledge. The more time that passes, the more readings you will be able to do and the easier it will be to understand what the cards have to tell us.

Before doing a reading, it is helpful to have some kind of "routine" and respect some "rules" that will help you concentrate and focus on the practice. Some good habits to adopt before a reading are:

- Be away from any distractions. If you can, turn your devices off (laptop, phone, TV, etc.). If you're living with someone, politely ask them not to disturb you while you're reading your cards.

- Do a cleansing practice to ensure you won't be affected by intrusive energies. Pick a place you feel comfortable, and cleanse the space, your-self, and the cards with incense (or by using any other cleansing methods that most suit you).

- Do a little meditation to ground yourself and increase your concentration. Lighting some candles or incense can help create a relaxing atmosphere. Try to clear your mind from intrusive thoughts and be present in the moment.

- If you have a connection to or work with a spirit, deity, angel, spirit animal, ancestor, or any other guidance, call them and kindly ask them to assist you in your reading.

- Be sure to have a pen and paper to write down your questions and answers so you can compare the messages from different readings in the future.

HOW TO READ THE CARDS
PICKING A SIGNIFICATOR:

The first step that many people like to take when starting a reading is picking a Significator. This card is usually picked purposefully; you can pick one that represents you best (or represents the person you're doing the reading for). You can base your choice on the zodiac sign, the elements, and the characteristics of that card.

Once you've found a card that best represents the subject of the reading, you must extract it from the deck and position it on the table, facing up. The other cards will then go near the Significator, facing down; we will review in detail the different tarot spreads in the last chapter. Picking the Significator is a great way to deepen your connection to the other cards to better understand their message.

Remember that this is not a fundamental step; you can choose to let the deck decide what the Significator will be, or you can do a reading following a precise spread, without a specific Significator.

READING REVERSED CARDS:

Before starting to shuffle the cards, it is important to know that not everyone feels comfortable reading reversed cards (cards that are dealt upside down). The reasons for this are many and often very different, depending on the tarot reader. Many think a reversed card does not indicate the opposite meaning from its straight counterpart (straight meaning "upright," rather than upside down), but rather conveys the same message on a smaller scale. In the next chapter, I explain both meanings: upright and reversed. You may decide to rely on the message of only upright cards or use both.

SHUFFLING THE DECK:

Now it's time to shuffle your deck; this may look like a quick step before your reading, but it is perhaps the most important. This is the moment where you connect with the cards and ask them your question. That's why it is essential to have a particular question in mind and ask it in the most specific and detailed way you can. Keep in mind that the more ambiguous and unclear the question is, the more unclear the answer will be.

While shuffling the cards, concentrate, pass your energy to the cards, and ask the question. Sometimes, while shuffling, a card might drop. This is a signal, a message that the cards are trying to send you. I always advise picking up the dropped card and looking for its meaning. Sometimes it could be a clear message of something that we never considered, it could be a warning, or it could be something that has nothing to do with our question but, for some reason, we need to know.

There's no right or wrong way to shuffle the cards; do what feels right to you and the cards will guide you to the answer.

CHAPTER
TWO

MINOR
ARCANA

THE MINOR ARCANA are 56 cards, 14 for each suit; they are mostly connected to the mundane world, to everyday life and its hidden aspects. They will show you struggles, interactions, behaviors, and thoughts and experiences you will face. They have an impermanent effect, as they reflect the energy that goes through your life, based on the action you decide to take.

THE SUIT OF WANDS

STRAIGHT: Willpower, passion

REVERSED: Aggression, volatility

ELEMENT: Fire

ASTROLOGY: Aries, Leo, Sagittarius

The Suit of Wands is often represented in colorful images, giving us a sense of vitality and enthusiasm. No matter how they're named (batons, clubs, staves, rods), they always have a phallic resemblance and that's because they represent the masculine energy and the element of fire, symbolizing energy, action, and orientation to success.

These cards speak to our creativity, skills, need for adventures, inspiration, and passion for life. They represent how we approach work and also our everyday challenges and willingness to take action.

On the other side, this passion can turn into something destructive when we find these cards reversed. We could see temperamental behaviors, recklessness, and aggression.

KING OF WANDS

This card reveals someone who can set goals and work until the desired results are achieved. We can see a determined man who knows what he wants and how to get it; the lion and salamander we see in the card are another way to show strength and power.

KING OF WANDS

STRAIGHT

You enjoy the energy of finding solutions for every problem and you're ready to take on any challenge. Your independence will bring you success as your enthusiasm will bring you trust and respect from other people.

IN A READING ABOUT LOVE: This card is a good sign that your hard work in your romantic life will pay off. You will be able to share your life with a creative and passionate person like yourself.

IN A READING ABOUT CAREER: There is a good chance you'll get a promotion or experience a big improvement in your career. Your hard work will bring you long-term results and success.

IN A READING ABOUT MONEY: Expect new income as your money-managing skills are strengthening your financial stability. Keep a balance between saving and spending to help others.

REVERSED

You might not find the support and stability you desire, and this is the result of arrogance, selfishness, and presumption. Maybe you don't have bad intentions; however, these traits are hurting you or someone else is hurting you.

IN A READING ABOUT LOVE: The pace of your love life might be slow; perhaps your behavior is what is pushing people away. Leave your partner space to express themselves and find their own solutions.

IN A READING ABOUT CAREER: Your projects might be evolving slowly; this could be because you're struggling to take the lead. Trust your intuition more than others' opinions.

IN A READING ABOUT MONEY: You won't receive as much money as you planned. Take control of your finances and take thoughtful actions.

QUEEN OF WANDS

The Queen of Wands is an authoritative figure that shows confidence and strength. It is rare for the Minor Arcana to depict a subject with a flower. Here, we can see her holding a sunflower, a sign of fertility and happiness; the wand is a sign of life. The Queen of Wands can signify warmth,

QUEEN OF WANDS

vibrant personalities, and fidelity, and when reversed, jealousy and greediness.

STRAIGHT

The person who this card is referring to is loving, loyal, respectful, and caring. It is a sign of being balanced and determined to bring the work that has been started to its conclusion. Similar to the King, she is an authoritative figure that is not scared to be the leader.

IN A READING ABOUT LOVE: There's a perfect balance between passion and commitment. Your strong personality and confidence make your relationships open and trustworthy.

IN A READING ABOUT CAREER: You have all the skills and energy to complete your projects and feel fulfilled. These great results will strengthen your talent and bring more possibilities.

IN A READING ABOUT MONEY: You're able to increase your finances by doing what you love; it is time to think bigger and make the next move.

REVERSED

Reversed, this card often brings drama caused by jealousy, manipulation, and lack of loyalty. Balancing wild emotions and using rationality is the best path to follow.

IN A READING ABOUT LOVE: There are aggressive emotions and a lack of caring in the air, whether it comes from you or your partner. Find the time to understand your needs and act accordingly.

IN A READING ABOUT CAREER: You don't have enthusiasm and lack initiative when it comes to your job. You feel drained and disconnected with what you do. Improving your mindset or changing your job is what will make you happier.

IN A READING ABOUT MONEY: Be careful when it comes to spending your money; before making a big decision, think carefully about the repercussions.

KNIGHT OF WANDS

This card is very clear and strict in its meaning. We see a young man riding his horse and wearing armor. In his expression, we can see determination; the flames and the salamanders on his armor show his strength and his preparedness for what is coming next.

KNIGHT OF WANDS

STRAIGHT

This card brings movement and it's a good sign to take a nice trip and to visit new places. It reveals enthusiasm for new adventures and projects, suggesting you keep energies high. As it brings something new, this card can also bring something unexpected; be ready for changes to come.

IN A READING ABOUT LOVE: Whether this represents a person or a situation, there's passion, vitality, and impulsivity that sometimes could be hard to deal with. Remember that free souls don't often like to settle down.

IN A READING ABOUT CAREER: You will travel for work and have the chance to visit new places. There could also be a lack of progress, but try to keep your passion and energy high.

IN A READING ABOUT MONEY: Unexpected money is coming your way; do not make an irrational purchase. Try to spend your money on a journey or something that expands your career.

REVERSED

This card reversed brings major delays and reveals the possible presence of someone who is not reliable. This could lead you to low self-esteem and frustration.

IN A READING ABOUT LOVE: Someone doesn't want to fully commit to the relationship. There's instability, confusion, and delays in the plans you made.

IN A READING ABOUT CAREER: There could be an unexpected change of job or delays for a trip. You're moving without a precise goal and that's what is causing you to feel unmotivated.

IN A READING ABOUT MONEY: You could be spending your money carelessly without thinking about the consequences. A possible loss of money is expected.

PAGE OF WANDS

A young, well-dressed man is observing the first blossoms from his wand; this is a representation of youth, and the enthusiasm that only young people have. Although he's not surrounded by a lot of vegetation (he has not achieved many results yet), his pure and kind heart can lead him to great accomplishments.

PAGE OF WANDS

STRAIGHT

This card signals excitement, curiosity about everything new, and the desire to succeed. The young age of the Page of Wands can show inexperience and also the possible inability to concretize. It reveals your drive for success but also some complications you'll have to deal with.

IN A READING ABOUT LOVE: You have an optimistic view of love and you will start a relationship with an open mind and heart. If you're single, it is the perfect moment to explore and meet new people.

IN A READING ABOUT CAREER: You're enjoying learning new skills and perhaps you are willing to learn a new job. It is a good time to welcome changes and new projects.

IN A READING ABOUT MONEY: There's some instability in your finances, as you could receive unexpected money and also lose some. Do not engage in impulsive buying and work toward more balance.

REVERSED

When reversed, we may have to consider the opposite of what was said for the upright Page of Wands. There's disappointment and an inability to make our ideas concrete. We might also find we've taken a risk in being around someone who cannot be trusted.

IN A READING ABOUT LOVE: This can bring childish behavior, infidelity, and lack of excitement. Spend some time thinking about what you want from a relationship, even if it means taking a break.

IN A READING ABOUT CAREER: You're feeling stuck, without a destination. This could be because of a lack of skills or motivation. It won't last forever as long as you start setting realistic goals and work toward them.

IN A READING ABOUT MONEY: There's a lack of stability, and one of the main reasons could be your easy spending. It could be helpful to learn how to save more money.

ACE OF WANDS

On this card we see a hand coming out of a cloud, holding a stick while a gentle wind surrounds it. This card tells us about the balance between spiritual and material worlds, and reminds us to keep an eye out for new opportunities, which is represented by the sprouts.

ACE OF WANDS

STRAIGHT

You have the perfect chance to reinvent yourself and start new projects and a new chapter. This is your moment to embrace your creativity and start that project that you have been waiting to begin.

IN A READING ABOUT LOVE: This can signal loyalty and long-term commitment if you're in a relationship, and a new romantic relationship if you're single. Flirting and passion will come to you easily.

IN A READING ABOUT CAREER: You are experiencing professional growth; your great creativity and ability to solve problems will take you far in your career. Stay focused and motivated.

IN A READING ABOUT MONEY: Your finances will significantly improve and you'll be able to resolve some financial issues. You might also receive a gift or unexpected income. However, this is not the right time for big spending.

REVERSED

There will be some delays in your projects despite your wanting to carry on with your creative ideas. There could be a sense of disorientation and you might feel unmotivated; this is because you don't know what to do. Think carefully about what you want to achieve and what you need to do to bring your vitality back.

IN A READING ABOUT LOVE: Although the relationship might be lovely, it may not be meant to last for long. In other cases, all that is required is better communication.

IN A READING ABOUT CAREER: You are feeling enthusiastic about your job; however, there will be issues and obstacles to overcome. Keep going and don't give up.

IN A READING ABOUT MONEY: It is not the time to invest, buy, or spend money in general. A decrease in your money is yet to come, so be prepared with some savings.

TWO OF WANDS

What grabs our attention in this card is the small globe that the man is holding. This particular representation means "having the world in your hands"; on the top of a castle, this man is wearing orange, which is connected with enthusiasm and hunger for life. He is ready for expansion, to engage in new adventures, and to make his dreams come true.

TWO OF WANDS

STRAIGHT

You're in a position where you've already spent time trying to figure out your goals and now you're ready to act, move forward, and enjoy the results. Your maturity and confidence in what you want are giving you the willingness to explore the world and embrace new experiences.

IN A READING ABOUT LOVE: You are ready to make some changes in your relationship, and because of that, open communication with your partner is essential.

IN A READING ABOUT CAREER: You know what you have to do and you're ready to take the ownership of your career. Let this card be another motivator to keep going and follow your plan.

IN A READING ABOUT MONEY: You have enough money to work toward stability and independence. It is time to stop depending on others and create some savings.

REVERSED

You have had a lack of goals for your future and perhaps too much arrogance. It is better to start thinking about your long-term life plans without depending on others.

IN A READING ABOUT LOVE: You'll have to be patient and accept that it is the right time to make plans, not enact them. You could be experiencing doubts and a lack of clear communication.

IN A READING ABOUT CAREER: You might have lost some control over your career. Working harder is required to accomplish your goals. Don't overthink too much, but take action.

IN A READING ABOUT MONEY: You won't get the financial reward you anticipated. This does not mean you will be broke, but be ready for unexpected troubles.

THREE OF WANDS

Three is often considered the perfect number. This affects the message of this card, as it encourages us to aim for satisfaction and achievement of our goals. The man in the card is observing what life has presented to him, thinking about what he needs to do to bring his dreams to life.

THREE OF WANDS

STRAIGHT

Now you have to do everything it takes to realize all your dreams; keep your mind open to new opportunities, which will massively improve your future. You have the means to show what you can do.

IN A READING ABOUT LOVE: It is the perfect time to take the next step: starting a new relationship, moving in together, or talking about marriage.

IN A READING ABOUT CAREER: You could forge a good partnership or just enjoy the results you're achieving. It is also a positive sign for business travel and exploring new places.

IN A READING ABOUT MONEY: Don't be afraid of spending, especially if it is to invest in your projects. Your hard work and financial stability will allow you to enjoy what you gained.

REVERSED

Despite your hard work and plans for the future, you might feel like you're not achieving everything you wanted. This does not mean all your work was pointless or that you won't have better opportunities in the future.

IN A READING ABOUT LOVE: Try not to force things on your partner or future partner; instead of hiding problems, it is better to check if both of you are committed and ready for a serious relationship.

IN A READING ABOUT CAREER: Some of your ideas are being rejected and this is making you feel frustrated. Even if things aren't going as planned, don't give up.

IN A READING ABOUT MONEY: There is some confusion in organizing your finances. You could lose some money or have payment delayed. It is better to be more in charge of your income.

FOUR OF WANDS

We can see a couple wearing laurel crowns in the middle of a ceremony. There is a festive atmosphere, and the couple is happy and joyful. It is time to celebrate your achievements and keep a positive mindset, even when some inconveniences occur.

FOUR OF WANDS

STRAIGHT

This card indicates a moment you can celebrate, spending time with your family and friends. This could be a wedding, a birthday, a promotion, or any event that you wish to celebrate.

IN A READING ABOUT LOVE: This card symbolizes family and community. If you're in a relationship, you have the support of those around you. Perhaps you're planning your wedding. If you're single, you could find love in your community.

IN A READING ABOUT CAREER: The Four of Wands represents fulfilment in your career and recognition for your abilities. You're making new connections and people appreciate your personality.

IN A READING ABOUT MONEY: You are profiting from your investments and your finances are secure and stable. You're free to enjoy your money and spend it on your family and friends.

REVERSED

This card reversed does not indicate an absence of achievements but more so an imbalance in your relationship with your family or friends. You are not receiving the support you desire and there could be disagreements and arguments.

IN A READING ABOUT LOVE: There are some problems between you and your partner and perhaps your family and friends. Tensions and possibly fear of taking the next step are affecting your mood. Everything can be solved with effort and communication.

IN A READING ABOUT CAREER: Relationships at work are getting harder. There are tensions, disagreements, and miscommunication. Expect some rude and selfish behaviors, but try to keep calm.

IN A READING ABOUT MONEY: Your finances are not in a bad place, but it's not the right time to spend large amounts of money or make big investments.

FIVE OF WANDS

On this card, five men are each holding their own sticks, waving them in the air, attempting to fight. It is not clear if the fight is a serious one or if they are just enjoying a playful battle. This card reveals competition, ambition, and tenacity, though not necessarily from anger and hate. Their

FIVE OF WANDS

faces are fairly relaxed and not scared or irritated.

STRAIGHT

There is some conflict resurfacing from the past or about to happen; this could be between you and a group of people where an agreement can't be found. This card could also indicate some sort of competition and rivalry between you and another person. The only solution is taking the first step to improve the communication.

IN A READING ABOUT LOVE: Different opinions and points of view can create arguments between you and your partner. If you're single you might be competing with other people interested in the same lover.

IN A READING ABOUT CAREER: Your job probably brings competition between colleagues and you always have to be ready to demonstrate your abilities. This could also indicate a temporary competition, perhaps for a new job. You have all the skills to succeed.

IN A READING ABOUT MONEY: Your financial instability is not meant to last forever; more work and patience is required. Expect some arguments or tension related to money.

REVERSED

Your way of dealing with troubles is pretending they are not there; this is making the problems bigger and you're feeling the tension now. This can also mean you just got out of an extremely stressful period of your life that was full of disputes.

IN A READING ABOUT LOVE: It is important to learn how to see other people's points of view without letting your ego take over. Honesty and an open mind can be the solution.

IN A READING ABOUT CAREER: An elevated sense of competition and unwillingness to cooperate is what you will find at your workplace. Perhaps you will be able to sort everything out, or you may start thinking about changing jobs.

IN A READING ABOUT MONEY: Depending on the context and which cards are combined with this one, it could mean you're finally getting out of a stressful period with your finances or that you will face intense arguments with family regarding money.

SIX OF WANDS

On this card there's a man wearing a wreath of victory and firmly holding a stick; the white horse is a sign of purity and success, while the crowd cheering the man from below is a symbol of celebration. Six is the number of balance between opposites, and in fact, this card is all about important

SIX OF WANDS

decisions: what we choose between good and evil, passion and rationality, right and wrong. It signals cheerfulness and pride in our achievements.

STRAIGHT

Not only have you been able to manage your skills and pursue your dreams, but you've also had the ability to obtain significant results. This card signals success, fulfilment, and recognition. People around you are joyful and proud of what you've done so far.

IN A READING ABOUT LOVE: This card indicates impending success and rewards. If you're single, people around you might find you attractive and see you with different eyes. If you're in a relationship, you will be able to take big steps forward.

IN A READING ABOUT CAREER: This card usually indicates self-confidence and rewards. You could receive a promotion or succeed in your projects. Always be careful to avoid letting your ego make you selfish.

IN A READING ABOUT MONEY: You're able to enjoy the results of your hard work and benefit from your financial stability. Don't get too confident though, as a few bad moves could ruin everything.

REVERSED

It is suggested you rethink your goals, and try to gain a better understanding of your situation and what you need. Sometimes your lack of confidence holds you back, and that's why it's good to be open to support.

IN A READING ABOUT LOVE: You or your partner are feeling neglected, not loved enough. Being open about your feelings is the best solution to fix the problem. If you're single, you might want to wait before you start dating.

IN A READING ABOUT CAREER: Egotistical behaviors are making your work harder to execute. You feel like you're not getting the recognition you deserve and that you're not capable of accomplishing your goals.

IN A READING ABOUT MONEY: You must take some time to plan your finances to avoid big losses. Keep being proactive and never let your guard down.

SEVEN OF WANDS

We are always given challenges to overcome, and that's part of life. The Seven of Wands shows a man defending himself from attacks from hidden people. His expression is defensive and his mismatching shoes are a sign of

SEVEN OF WANDS

disorganization. Seven is the symbol of completeness and alignment, both aspects that are achievable through self-preservation.

STRAIGHT

This card shows all the struggles and challenges we have to face in life to maintain our position, whatever that is. You must hold your ground and keep pursuing your dreams, even when others try to slow you down.

IN A READING ABOUT LOVE: You might be thinking about giving up, but this card suggests that you keep trying to fix your issues, always respecting your boundaries.

IN A READING ABOUT CAREER: Keep working toward your goals and don't let distractions slow you down. If you keep staying focused, you'll have good results.

IN A READING ABOUT MONEY: You might have to deal with others' jealousy and arguments about money. Keep working on your finances no matter what and reinforce your stability.

REVERSED

You're unsure what to do to bring more balance into your life. Confusion and indecision are taking over. Try to find healing when experiencing aggressive emotions and the thought of giving up.

IN A READING ABOUT LOVE: It is getting more and more difficult for you and your partner to stay together. This could be the result of too much defensiveness from you or too many external opinions. Perhaps therapy or an open talk can help.

IN A READING ABOUT CAREER: Pay attention to who's jealous of you and trying to make you fail. You have to learn to defend yourself and your work.

IN A READING ABOUT MONEY: Although your finances are not in a bad place, you're engaging in too much unnecessary spending. It is best to save money and buy less.

EIGHT OF WANDS

There are eight wands hurtling through the air, going to a precise destination. The weather is good and the water flows freely, which means there aren't complications. The card suggests action, movement, and new beginnings.

EIGHT OF WANDS

STRAIGHT

The problems we saw in the Seven of Wands are now over; your effort is stabilizing the energies and it's finally time to move forward. Exciting news is coming, so you should look toward the future with enthusiasm. Act on your desires and remember that there is no space for distractions.

IN A READING ABOUT LOVE: A new love is coming, bringing excitement, romance, and frantic energy. If you're in a relationship, be ready to spice things up and find more adventure.

IN A READING ABOUT CAREER: Things are moving fast. This could bring a promotion, a higher wage, or a business trip. Keep your confidence up and enjoy the moment.

IN A READING ABOUT MONEY: You're feeling like a quick decision must be made and the outcome might be out of your hands. This could be either positive or negative; just remember that having control over your finances is essential.

REVERSED

The large number of activities and changes in your life could be overwhelming. Your past decisions could have a negative impact on you, but now is the time to let go and find new solutions.

IN A READING ABOUT LOVE: This card can bring a lot of misunderstandings. Whether you're in a relationship or not, be wary of upcoming intense discussions and stressful moments.

IN A READING ABOUT CAREER: This card can mean you're moving too fast or that you're not moving fast enough. A sense of stagnation will make you think you're not achieving anything. Sometimes asking for external help is beneficial.

IN A READING ABOUT MONEY: You're feeling like your income is not enough and despite your work, your finances are not where you'd like them to be. Your work will pay off if you stay consistent.

NINE OF WANDS

The man depicted looks rough, injured, and tired. The way he's holding his stick is a sign that he's still ready to battle and defend himself. This card encapsulates a mixture of battles to fight, strength, victory, and hope.

NINE OF WANDS

STRAIGHT

Even though you will be facing challenges and perhaps be betrayed by someone close to you, you will have the power to get through this hard time. This card signals hope, willpower, and encouragement. Don't be afraid of making bold moves, as the resulting surprise might be a pleasant one.

IN A READING ABOUT LOVE: You will be able to solve past issues and get closer to your partner. You are ready to take big steps and embrace new beginnings.

IN A READING ABOUT CAREER: Your work has been stressful recently and you're not quite done with the struggles. Despite that, you're halfway to success—keep working hard.

IN A READING ABOUT MONEY: You're not in a bad position, but at the same time, your finances are not stable. It is not advised that you touch your savings; instead, you might seek an additional source of income.

REVERSED

A particular situation is causing you stress and preventing you from being yourself. You, however, are trying to avoid facing the issue, and this could cause low confidence and more problems. Learn from your past mistakes and find the power within.

IN A READING ABOUT LOVE: There are a lot of unresolved issues, and there are two possible solutions: find a compromise or end the relationship. If you're single, your behavior could keep people away from you.

IN A READING ABOUT CAREER: This could be your time to change course and explore a twist in your career. If you feel drained and exhausted, it is best to change tactics and adopt different behaviors.

IN A READING ABOUT MONEY: You need to be more aware of and responsible for your finances. Irresponsible spending or avoiding problems will make your situation worse.

TEN OF WANDS

Here we observe a man carrying a large amount of weight. The wands he is holding seem too heavy, and he seems to be struggling. Despite the struggle, the man is still going and his strength will allow him to arrive to his destination.

TEN OF WANDS

STRAIGHT

It is very common for people to carry too many responsibilities and duties on their shoulders; it's easy to feel burnout and exhaustion as a result of our life and our surroundings. It is not time to give up, but better management of our energy is needed to accomplish our goals.

IN A READING ABOUT LOVE: External factors like work or people are making it hard for you to focus on romance. Don't be afraid to talk about it with your partner or ask for some alone time.

IN A READING ABOUT CAREER: Your work is overwhelming you with responsibilities and tasks. Your energy is very low, and that's why you shouldn't be scared of asking for help or perhaps time off.

IN A READING ABOUT MONEY: There is a big burden on your shoulders that could be present in many different scenarios. If you can't find a solution by yourself, it is best to seek professional advice.

REVERSED

You are carrying too much on your shoulders, and this could involve other people's problems as well. This stress is unnecessary in your life and it is best to get rid of it and focus more on yourself.

IN A READING ABOUT LOVE: You and your partner are not sharing all the problems you are experiencing. Asking for help and being open is always the best choice.

IN A READING ABOUT CAREER: You don't have to deal with major issues anymore, whether you managed to resolve them or not. It is time to rest and remember that self-care is important.

IN A READING ABOUT MONEY: This could mean that you are finally free from the problems that were affecting your finances or that you ignored them; if it's the latter, you could be expecting big losses.

THE SUIT OF CUPS

STRAIGHT: Emotions, relationships

REVERSED: Emotional blockages, repression

ELEMENT: Water

ASTROLOGY: Cancer, Scorpio, Pisces

The Suits of Cups is connected to water and all the characteristics that come with it; we will be talking about intuition, emotions, and how we feel about and treat people.

These cards carry feminine energy and forces inspired by their shape, which remind us of a womb. These cards encapsulate how we express our feelings and how we are able to care for others and ourselves. That is why we will see many depictions of people expressing their emotions—whether they be joy or sadness—channeled with creativity and elements of self-expression.

When reversed, these cards could symbolize being so trapped within our bubble of emotions that we are almost detached from the real world. They could bring repression and emotional and creative blockages.

KING OF CUPS

The King of Cups is a card that brings emotional balance and kindness despite its authoritative look. The fish-shaped amulet that the King is wearing shows his creativity. The fish jumping out of the water in the background on the left and the ship on the right represent the balance between emotional and material worlds.

KING OF CUPS

STRAIGHT

You are highly sensitive, creative, and have the ability to understand emotions and logic at the same time. Although you can be controlling at home, you're also understanding and kind.

IN A READING ABOUT LOVE: You're able to balance love and logic, intuition and passion. Your calm mind will get you through any stressful situation; the love you give is the love you receive.

IN A READING ABOUT CAREER: Your mental balance is able to bring you peace, even in your workplace. This is why others respect and admire you. This could also mean you are meant to pursue a creative career.

IN A READING ABOUT MONEY: Your finances are stable, but you risk losing your stability. Always remember to use both intuition and rationality.

REVERSED

This card reversed can indicate manipulation, deception, and inability to express emotions. You may have irrational feelings and carelessness regarding unhealthy behaviors. This could be related to someone in your life or something within you.

IN A READING ABOUT LOVE: You are experiencing selfishness and a lack of commitment. This could lead to manipulative behaviors and apathy.

IN A READING ABOUT CAREER: There could be a tyrannical boss at your work who doesn't care about anyone's needs, or this could indicate your sense of being unfulfilled.

IN A READING ABOUT MONEY: Decisions based only on your emotions and a lack of real interest are making your finances insecure.

QUEEN OF CUPS

The woman depicted in this card is the embodiment of the beauty of emotions; she's holding a closed cup, which symbolizes her subconscious emotions. The sea beneath her is calm, reflecting her feelings and subconscious. Her feet are not touching the water, but the ground, which means she's watching her emotions from the outside. The calm atmosphere shows how peaceful she is.

QUEEN OF CUPS

STRAIGHT

This card shows a very compassionate, intuitive, and kind person—someone who is able to read people's emotions and has a strong inner voice to guide them. You are helping others and supporting them with loving acts.

IN A READING ABOUT LOVE: Your loving personality and kind heart attract many people. Some might be nice but others could drain all your energy. Be cautious about who you choose.

IN A READING ABOUT CAREER: This card could be telling you that your ability to care for others can benefit you and your career. However, it could also mean that money is not everything, and that you should be focused on your spiritual self as well.

IN A READING ABOUT MONEY: You are able to spend your money to care for others; do not worry about what comes of this too much, as money is not the most important thing.

REVERSED

You're experiencing instability and a lack of knowledge regarding how to manage all your emotions. Being hypersensitive or too fearful can cause confusion and make it impossible to solve any issue.

IN A READING ABOUT LOVE: You're the one who puts more effort into the relationship, and that is not healthy. There is an environment of tension and stress. Infidelity might occur as well.

IN A READING ABOUT CAREER: You're feeling emotionally exhausted and work is putting a lot of pressure on you. Take time to think about what makes you truly happy and work toward that.

IN A READING ABOUT MONEY: Your emotional state is reflected in your spending habits. Always go to the root of the problem and focus on saving instead of spending.

KNIGHT OF CUPS

A young knight is proudly and slowly riding his horse, holding a cup, almost as if he has to deliver it to someone. There is a sense of calm and tranquility, contrary to the Knights of Swords and Wands. The white horse is a symbol of spirituality and purity, while the winged helmet shows imagination and creativity.

KNIGHT OF CUPS

STRAIGHT

This is the card that most shows the connection with intuition, calmness, and consciousness. The Knight is in tune with his emotions, and his personality makes him attractive and interesting to others. He's able to connect with the feminine forces, listen to his intuition, and act accordingly. This card also suggests that we embrace romance, creativity, and our deepest feelings.

IN A READING ABOUT LOVE: Expect a passionate and romantic relationship to come into your life. Remember though—being too romantic and unrealistic won't allow it to last long.

IN A READING ABOUT CAREER: Your calm mind enables you find solutions to most problems and your logic is helping you succeed. This card can also encourage you to start a creative job.

IN A READING ABOUT MONEY: Some moments of reflection, talking, and creativity are needed to resolve any possible issues. This way your finances will continue to stay stable.

REVERSED

There is difficulty in commitment and keeping promises; insecurities and indecisions are strong and affect reality. You could be feeling jealous, impulsive, and moody.

IN A READING ABOUT LOVE: There are a lot of empty promises. Romance can turn into lies and irresponsibility. Be aware of this pattern— sometimes it is better to stay alone.

IN A READING ABOUT CAREER: This could mean there are large disagreements at work; you're not handling your emotions very well, or perhaps your need for peace could turn into unhealthy behavior. You need to find the balance between your different moods.

IN A READING ABOUT MONEY: Your actions are not effective and what you planned might not happen. Make sure you know what the best move is to make some improvements.

PAGE OF CUPS

A young man, clothed in a floral dress, is about to drink from his cup with an elegant bearing. Suddenly, a fish comes out of his cup, and instead of drinking what's inside, the young man has to face the fish. It looks almost as if the fish has something to tell him. The message behind this card is a reminder of the unexpected inspiration that comes without warnings, straight from the unconscious.

PAGE OF CUPS

STRAIGHT

A wave of creativity is coming, and you should be ready to welcome it, express your ideas, and engage in artistic activities. If you've recently felt like giving up on your dreams, this card is telling you to keep pursuing them. Even during disputes, do not suppress your feelings—let them out without fear.

IN A READING ABOUT LOVE: You are emotional, creative, and almost naive when it comes to love. If you're in a relationship, you might see your partner with new eyes and discover new elements of who they are; if you're single, a shy and romantic love is about to start.

IN A READING ABOUT CAREER: You do best in creative and artistic jobs; you have issues related to putting your emotions out into the world and often your head is in the clouds. Follow your dreams even if it requires hard work.

IN A READING ABOUT MONEY: Your goals could be too unrealistic. It is better to grow your income step by step.

REVERSED

You could be going through some creative and emotional blockages; there's a sense of apathy and inability to express your emotions. Self-love and self-esteem are low; this can sometimes turn into addiction to drugs and alcohol.

IN A READING ABOUT LOVE: There is insecurity and immaturity in managing emotions. Someone is being shy and complicated to deal with. Be aware of these traits and decide if you can deal with them.

IN A READING ABOUT CAREER: You're having a hard time overcoming your blockages; your emotional volatility is causing you to be unprofessional and struggle to manage your feelings at work.

IN A READING ABOUT MONEY: Don't let your emotions affect your income; face your problems instead of avoiding them.

ACE OF CUPS

This card does not have space for a human figure—instead, it is full of symbols. There's a hand popping out of a cloud, holding the Graal, the sacred cup of spiritual regeneration. It reveals that something unexpected is coming, something we were waiting for for a long time and that we thought

ACE OF CUPS

would never happen. The dove is a symbol of peace, while the four streams of water are symbols of the power of our intuition and inner voice.

STRAIGHT

You're living life to the fullest. A new adventure is starting; it could be a creative one or a new romance. Either way, it's going to be filled with love and joy.

IN A READING ABOUT LOVE: This card indicates a lot of love and happiness. If you're single, you will start a loving relationship soon;

if you're already in one, expect to discover new emotions and welcome a fierce passion.

IN A READING ABOUT CAREER: A new job, a new project, or a new professional relationship could come into your life. It is the right time to take on new challenges and follow your creativity.

IN A READING ABOUT MONEY: The friendly element of this card will allow you to receive the support that you need to increase your finances.

REVERSED

The Ace of Cups reversed indicates closure, negativity, and the opposite of all the Graal's qualities. Even in good moments, we could experience problems and stress. Although this is a hard card, our actions can always change the situation.

IN A READING ABOUT LOVE: You could experience a breakup or some difficult arguments. There's sadness and a temporary lack of love. Listen to your inner voice and find love within.

IN A READING ABOUT CAREER: You won't have good luck in finding a new job or getting a promotion. There's a lack of creativity and motivation. Do not let this moment ruin your days.

You might not receive the help you expected or you could feel unmotivated and unable to make changes.

TWO OF CUPS

There are two young figures—a man and a woman—exchanging their cups as a sign of support, one that could be related to love, friendship, or work. Above them, there is the symbol of Hermes, who represents negotiation, protection, cosmic energy, and duality. On top of it, there's a chimaera, the symbol of partnership and passion.

TWO OF CUPS

STRAIGHT

You and your partner are experiencing harmony, mutual respect, and support in every aspect of your relationship. This relationship is based on mutual love, trust, and affinity.

IN A READING ABOUT LOVE: This card shows harmony, love, and affinity in the relationship. It is a happy moment where everything is going smoothly.

IN A READING ABOUT CAREER: There is a happy and harmonious relationship; this could be between colleagues, a new partnership that will improve your career, or perhaps a romantic affinity with someone at work.

IN A READING ABOUT MONEY: Although you're not about to see big returns, you still have stable finances and income. However, be careful not to spend too much money on unnecessary things.

REVERSED

A relationship is about to fall apart, as the two forces that once attracted one another are now creating separation. Try to get to the core of the problems—there's a chance you can find a solution.

IN A READING ABOUT LOVE: There could be an intense codependency that causes tensions and arguments. Remember to give importance to individuality and be open to resolving problems.

IN A READING ABOUT CAREER: The people you're working with are not understanding your ideas and needs. There is difficulty in finding agreement and harmony.

IN A READING ABOUT MONEY: There's a lot of instability when it comes to your money. You might be spending too much and not caring about the losses. It is time to take a step back and resolve this situation.

THREE OF CUPS

Three women are celebrating together, holding their chalices upward; in this card, there's celebration, growth, dynamism, and expansion. The wreaths on their heads show victory, and the field full of flowers is a symbol of joy.

THREE OF CUPS

STRAIGHT

You're enjoying your bond with the people you love, expressing your joy, admiration, and creativity. This could also represent meeting old friends or a ceremony like a wedding, a birthday, or a baptism.

IN A READING ABOUT LOVE: A friend could turn into your new lover or you could find new love thanks to your social life. If you are in a relationship, it is a good moment to spend time with family, friends, and your partner.

IN A READING ABOUT CAREER: It is time for celebration, whether that is because of a promotion, a changing of jobs, or finishing school. Your workplace is peaceful and you have good relationships with your colleagues.

IN A READING ABOUT MONEY: Partnership with other people or investment will bring you prosperity. Enjoy it and spend your money without wasting it.

REVERSED

There could be a crisis or struggle in a relationship on the horizon. This card is not a negative card; we can think of it as a weaker upright Three of Cups. You'll find imbalance in your social life and difficulties in relating to people.

IN A READING ABOUT LOVE: You might feel lonely, with little time to spend with your friends and family. You might deal with some gossip or short-lived relationships.

IN A READING ABOUT CAREER: Whatever you planned in the past weeks or months could be delayed; your workplace could be unhealthy, as well as your relationship with your colleagues. Try not to let it affect you too much.

IN A READING ABOUT MONEY: You are worried about your financial situation. Perhaps you had to spend a big amount of money recently and now you're at a loss. It is advised that you plan for the future.

FOUR OF CUPS

A young man sits by a tree on a top of a mountain, away from everyone; he seems to be pensive, in a meditative state. He is so concentrated that he's not aware of the hand offering him a chalice, and he's also unimpressed by the other three chalices in front of him. This is telling us that

FOUR OF CUPS

sometimes we are not grateful for what we have. The solution is often in front of us but we can't see it.

STRAIGHT

You're probably going through a period of stagnation and lack of motivation, where everything seems to be going nowhere. You have some introspective work to do. Try to find the thing that sparks your creativity and happiness, and be more in touch with your inner self.

IN A READING ABOUT LOVE: You have little interest in the world of love and romance. This might be because you're not ready for a relationship or because you're trying to protect yourself.

IN A READING ABOUT CAREER: Your work is boring you and making you feel like you're not achieving anything. You can't focus or commit. You need to ask yourself: What is the next step I need to take to be happier?

IN A READING ABOUT MONEY: You're not mentally connected to your finances, and illusions can worsen the situation. Gratitude and awareness can be the solution.

REVERSED

In this case, the reversed card could be considered more positive than the upright version. After a period of apathy, you're suddenly feeling the need to be more aware and more connected to what's in front of you. Try not to miss the chances that life is presenting to you.

IN A READING ABOUT LOVE: You're slowly letting go of the past and pain you had inside. It is time to be excited about the future and what love can bring you.

IN A READING ABOUT CAREER: You'll suddenly find the right motivation to release your sense of stagnation and find your lost creativity. Your actions are key if you want to unlock big achievements.

You're slowly getting back on track and your finances are recovering. Stay focused to gain more stability.

FIVE OF CUPS

It is rare in the Minor Arcana to find such a dark and gloomy card. We can see a person wearing a black cloak, and although we can't see his face, his posture gives a sense of despair. He's focusing on the three overturned cups, without noticing the two straight cups behind him. The river represents his tormented emotions, which are separating him from his home.

FIVE OF CUPS

STRAIGHT

There is sadness and a mixture of dark feelings; this card encourages us to leave the past behind, learn from our mistakes, and look forward to the future.

IN A READING ABOUT LOVE: You're going through a hard breakup or difficult emotions. Although you're feeling down, the future will offer you positive opportunities.

IN A READING ABOUT CAREER: You might have lost your job or a good opportunity; there is loss and grief, which are part of a big transformation. Try to stay positive and look at the bright side.

IN A READING ABOUT MONEY: You will probably suffer a big loss, so this is not the best time for big investments. Stay positive, as good things can still happen in the future.

REVERSED

You are learning how to accept your past and all the negativity that you experienced. You're letting go of what was causing you pain and learning from your mistakes.

IN A READING ABOUT LOVE: You're seeing the light at the end of the tunnel. It is time to start a new chapter by letting go of past issues, whether you're single or in a relationship.

IN A READING ABOUT CAREER: You're overcoming the stress and sadness that your job or previous job has given you. After a long period of imbalance, you're now recovering.

IN A READING ABOUT MONEY: You're slowly finding solutions to recover your past losses. Keep being positive and grateful for what you're achieving.

SIX OF CUPS

A young man is passing a cup full of flowers to a little girl. All the cups are full of flowers, which give us a sense of joy. There is the past, represented by the young man, gently giving space to the present, the little girl. It is a friendly encounter, a moment of peace after a long battle,

SIX OF CUPS

where they both understand that they will always coexist, but at the same time, must be focused on the here and now.

STRAIGHT

You are welcoming happy times, letting old memories warm your heart; you might be going back to a familiar place or trying to find answers in your past. You are also finding love in the people who surround you.

IN A READING ABOUT LOVE: You're healing from past traumas, letting good memories put a smile on your face. Old memories and perhaps people from your past are bringing you happiness.

IN A READING ABOUT CAREER: You are looking at your past job as a great lesson you can use to improve. Sometimes this could also mean thinking of going back to an old workplace.

IN A READING ABOUT MONEY: You are receiving support from your family or old friends, strengthening your stability. This could also mean sharing your expenses with other people.

REVERSED

There's a deep instability, vulnerability, and unwillingness to let go of the past. Although it is good to remember our past experiences, we will not be able to see what the future has to offer us if we're only looking backward.

IN A READING ABOUT LOVE: A more mature approach to your relationships is needed. Let go of past experiences and give more space to those who are around you now.

IN A READING ABOUT CAREER: Choosing an old, stable job, especially if it doesn't make you happy, could be an unhealthy choice. Release old patterns and give space to a new version of yourself.

IN A READING ABOUT MONEY: Your finances are becoming more stable, and that's why it's time for more independence. If you're living at home, it is time to leave the nest and start a new chapter.

SEVEN OF CUPS

SEVEN OF CUPS

Here we have a man who looks surprised at what he's seeing. The clouds represent imagination and dreams, while the seven cups hold seven different images, showing that we have to be careful what we wish for and always look beyond illusions.

STRAIGHT

You might have to choose between different options and you're unsure what to pick; be careful what you wish for and do not waste too much time fantasizing. Concrete actions are as important as dreaming.

IN A READING ABOUT LOVE: You might be presented with many temptations and you're unsure of what to do. Follow your instincts and be wary of any red flags.

IN A READING ABOUT CAREER: You're in a good place where you can pick between many good options; keep your confidence high and analyze every possible consequence.

IN A READING ABOUT MONEY: You have many ways to improve your finances—however, illusions could trick you. Keep your eyes open when it's time to make a decision.

REVERSED

The meaning of this card is not too far from the upright version. However, here we can see the more negative side. Dreaming too much and living in illusions is making you detached from reality. This can also mean the end of illusions and daydreaming.

IN A READING ABOUT LOVE: Your lack of clarity is stopping you from making important decisions. Take your next step without wasting too much time.

IN A READING ABOUT CAREER: You feel like there are no opportunities to improve your career. Take this time to set new goals and work toward them.

IN A READING ABOUT MONEY: This could bring the ability to be in charge of your finances and find new solutions, and it could also show that you have an unwillingness to face reality. Find a realistic way to improve your income.

EIGHT OF CUPS

We can see a person leaving everything behind, tired of what the eight cups have to offer him. This is a representation of transformation and transition, a need to find joy in the unknown and leave behind what we are familiar with.

EIGHT OF CUPS

STRAIGHT

This card shows how your everyday life and your routine are not benefitting you anymore. You're about to begin a transformation within yourself; you're seeking new adventures and new stimulation, leaving your past behind.

IN A READING ABOUT LOVE: It is time to consider if you want to be in a relationship and you're ready for commitment or if you're just scared of being on your own. The answer is within.

IN A READING ABOUT CAREER: You need some time off and perhaps some alone time. It could be a holiday, some days off, or just a simple walk away from work.

IN A READING ABOUT MONEY: Try to take a step back and look at your finances objectively. Learn what you need to do to improve them and think about future plans.

REVERSED

You're searching for new beginnings, but at the same time, you're scared of walking away from an old situation to start a new life. This inner crisis can be helpful if you spend time thinking about what you really want.

IN A READING ABOUT LOVE: You have a desire to be on your own and you're scared to leave your relationship. Think about why you're feeling this way and act accordingly.

IN A READING ABOUT CAREER: You want to leave your job and have more freedom but you're scared of the consequences. Sometimes changes are needed to regain joy.

IN A READING ABOUT MONEY: You're afraid of abandoning old sources of income for new ones. This can be a slow, transformative process that will bring you better results.

NINE OF CUPS

Here we see a middle-aged man sitting on a wooden bench, with a content expression and his arms crossed. Nine cups are in line behind him, all well positioned. We can see the man's gratification in accomplishing all his goals, and in his spiritual and material fulfilment.

NINE OF CUPS

STRAIGHT

After a long period of struggle and ups and downs, you can finally take a breath and enjoy what you achieved. This is a good luck card, as it is a sign that your dreams are coming true.

IN A READING ABOUT LOVE: There are many things to celebrate when it comes to your love life. You are open to receiving a loving and happy romantic relationship.

IN A READING ABOUT CAREER: Your hard work is paying off and you're getting some recognition. People at work are looking at you with new eyes and that's why you should take advantage of this situation.

IN A READING ABOUT MONEY: You're able to gain everything you wish for. There's abundance and wealth coming your way. Enjoy this moment.

REVERSED

Your desires are not turning into reality, and you might be experiencing solitude and disappointment. Maybe your goals weren't the right ones and perhaps you recently acted greedily. Be grateful for what you have in life and pay more attention to family and friends.

IN A READING ABOUT LOVE: Your relationship is not in a bad place, but you're not feeling fulfilled. This is because you need to work on your inner self to truly enjoy what's around you.

IN A READING ABOUT CAREER: You are not feeling satisfied and you feel like all your goals are becoming harder to accomplish. It is time to rethink your strategy.

IN A READING ABOUT MONEY: Your financial habits are not giving you the results you were hoping for. Do not be too negative, and work on possible solutions.

TEN OF CUPS

This happy picture shows two adults enjoying their happy place, with their arms in the air. There's a little house surrounded by nature. The river shows the flowing of emotions, while the cups form a rainbow, a symbol of blessings.

TEN OF CUPS

STRAIGHT

You're happy and proud of what you have achieved. You're experiencing harmony between you and your family and friends. There's a sense of fulfilment, joy, and gratitude for everything you have in your life.

IN A READING ABOUT LOVE: Your partner and your family are part of a happy environment, filled with love and respect. If you're single, you're about to find a long-lasting love.

IN A READING ABOUT CAREER: You found opportunities to grow professionally while cultivating a good environment with your colleagues. You have enough time to spend with your family and friends.

IN A READING ABOUT MONEY: You might have a lot of income coming your way, and you feel happy and grateful for what you have.

REVERSED

You might have some issues to solve with your family, as they are causing you too much stress. There's disappointment and a lack of fulfilment in your environment. Chose love over arguments—this is the only way to get harmony back.

IN A READING ABOUT LOVE: Your family might be causing problems between you and your partner. Ensure stability in your relationship.

IN A READING ABOUT CAREER: The atmosphere at work is not welcoming and that's making you feel uncomfortable and discouraged. This card can also reveal overworking.

IN A READING ABOUT MONEY: There could be financial instability in your family and that's causing stress. Working on the emotional imbalance can be part of the solution.

THE SUIT OF PENTACLES

STRAIGHT: Money, stability

REVERSED: Greediness, carelessness

ELEMENT: Earth

ASTROLOGY: Taurus, Virgo, Capricorn

The Suit of Pentacles is connected to the earth, and therefore is all about stability and reliability. We can find many names for this type of card, such as coins, stars, pentagrams, or discs.

In the past, it was commonly associated with mercenaries, trading, and labor. As such, the main topics will be money, the material world, how we feel and act in money-related situations, and how we behave in the mundane world.

While the reversed pentagram is often misinterpreted, in this case it is all about instability, being too attached to materialistic things, and being possessive and careless.

KING OF PENTACLES

The King is depicted as an authoritative person who exercises a lot of power; he has wealth, prosperity, and every imaginable materialistic resource. His life is luxurious, and the castle behind him shows determination.

KING OF PENTACLES

STRAIGHT

You have built their success from nothing or you are about to welcome prosperity and wealth. There is no selfishness, as the King provides for people and shares everything he has. There's a sense of security and stability.

IN A READING ABOUT LOVE: After hard work, there's stability, constant love, and commitment. Enjoy this beautiful moment and try not to miss a beat.

IN A READING ABOUT CAREER: This is the perfect card to ensure success in business. You can either achieve success on your own or find a good mentor who will help you along the way.

IN A READING ABOUT MONEY: You've worked very hard and now your finances are secure and stable. Not only can you enjoy your money, but you also have the opportunity to share it and help others.

REVERSED

There's a person, whether you or someone else, who has based their entire life on material things: money, success, work. There isn't an interest in helping others, in spending time nurturing relationships and creating bonds. This could also be someone who will soon become your enemy.

IN A READING ABOUT LOVE: Pay attention to people who use their possessions to exert control over others. There is someone in your life who is selfish, heartless, and unreliable.

IN A READING ABOUT CAREER: There could be someone trying to discourage you, or this could mean a lack of success in business and perhaps the end of a project.

IN A READING ABOUT MONEY: There will be a financial loss that will significantly impact your life. This could also mean you're being stingy and selfish.

QUEEN OF PENTACLES

The Queen of Pentacles is sitting on a throne full of animalistic figures: a goat, an angel, and other hidden symbols of sexual pleasure and materialistic abundance. The nature around her is another symbol of abundance, while the rabbit beneath is a sign of fertility.

QUEEN OF PENTACLES

STRAIGHT

This card reveals a motherly figure rooted in the earth, able to find solutions, give love, and achieve financial success. She encourages independence, strength, and the keeping of sound principles.

IN A READING ABOUT LOVE: You are focused on a relationship, enjoying sexual pleasure and creating a stable life. Your relationship or future one is (or will be) able to give you everything you need.

IN A READING ABOUT CAREER: You—or you with the help of a mentor—will find success and a fruitful career. Use all your skills to get to where you want to be.

IN A READING ABOUT MONEY: Although hard work is required, this card signals abundance, stability, and wealth.

REVERSED

This card reversed shows laziness, jealousy, and manipulative behavior. There is an inability to manage money and other possessions, as well as a manifestation of negativity as a result of excessive attachment to material things.

IN A READING ABOUT LOVE: You or your partner is full of insecurities, jealousy, and unresolved issues. If you're in a relationship, consider whether it could be too unhealthy. If you're single, you need more time to work on yourself before engaging in a new relationship.

IN A READING ABOUT CAREER: There is a colleague or a partner who is slowing your work down and there could be some jealousy. Be aware of possible evil intentions coming from those around you.

IN A READING ABOUT MONEY: Money can't resolve all problems. It is advised that you work on your attachment to material things and focus on the inner work you have to do.

KNIGHT OF PENTACLES

KNIGHT OF PENTACLES

The Knight is sitting on his horse. He's not going anywhere, as he is just focusing on one coin. This card represents thinking carefully about the future, being pensive and calculating about what needs to be done. Rationality and a sense of responsibility will guide your instincts.

STRAIGHT

You're focused on all your duties and are very committed to being reliable and staying on track. You know exactly what you're doing and have a clear sense of all your goals.

IN A READING ABOUT LOVE: You have encountered someone trustworthy, respectful, and loyal. Although the sense of romance might not be very strong, it is still a stable and loving relationship.

IN A READING ABOUT CAREER: You're dedicated to your work and you're ready to work hard to achieve your goals. If you're looking for a job, be ready to prove your abilities.

IN A READING ABOUT MONEY: You're good at saving money and planning your finances to work toward a better future. Remember to also enjoy what you're gaining.

REVERSED

Your daily routine is making you feel bored and unmotivated. Perhaps this is the time to try to do things differently to regain your zest for life. Sometimes the best solution is to embrace more spirituality and less materialistic activities.

IN A READING ABOUT LOVE: You are enjoying being on your own more than being with someone else. If you're in a relationship, maybe it's worth introducing some changes to spark your routine.

IN A READING ABOUT CAREER: This could mean you're not working hard enough to get your dream job, letting discouragement cloud your days. Remember to enjoy life in addition to thinking about your career.

IN A READING ABOUT MONEY: You need to find more balance between spending money and saving it. Focus on patience and organization.

PAGE OF PENTACLES

PAGE OF PENTACLES

A young man is in a beautiful field, full of vegetation and tranquility. He is very focused on his coin, showing devotion and loyalty. This card is all about being grounded and dedicated to our objectives. It symbolizes success, sensuality, prosperity, and wealth.

STRAIGHT

You're full of energy, ready to commit to a new project and find passion for it. You have a great entrepreneurial spirit that allows you to expand your abilities and work toward your desires.

IN A READING ABOUT LOVE: You are very ambitious, loyal, and dedicated to the relationship as well as their goals. You are a serious and hard worker but also funny and creative.

IN A READING ABOUT CAREER: You're good at planning your goals, always studying to learn more and working hard. You're building a strong foundation for your future—keep your motivation high.

IN A READING ABOUT MONEY: Expect to receive good news about your finances. Always plan how to spend your money and how to invest it.

REVERSED

You're struggling to keep your attention on daily tasks and your goals; you could be feeling lazy, depressed, and low-energy. Try to take a break to take care of yourself and find clarity about what you want to do.

IN A READING ABOUT LOVE: A relationship could be monotonous and lacking passion. There's a lack of commitment and enthusiasm. Hard work is needed to improve the situation.

IN A READING ABOUT CAREER: You could feel unprepared when it comes to your career, and you're struggling to work toward your future. Being more realistic about what your goals are can be helpful, in addition to welcoming spirituality into your life.

IN A READING ABOUT MONEY: Bad news is coming, whether it's about a loss or your excessive spending. It is better to learn how to save and find more stability.

ACE OF PENTACLES

A big hand is coming out from a cloud, holding a gold coin with an engraved pentagram. This symbolizes wealth, prosperity, and stability found in material possessions. The flourishing garden shows growth and fertility, while the distant mountains are a sign of ambition.

ACE OF PENTACLES

STRAIGHT

This card reveals new financial possibilities. This could be a new project, a new business idea, or a new job. Now is the time to plant your seeds for wealth. Be sure to be realistic and focus on what you're doing.

IN A READING ABOUT LOVE: This kind of relationship is full of abundance and stability; there's love, respect, and loyalty. If you're single, make sure to focus on your practical life as well.

IN A READING ABOUT CAREER: You will receive new proposals and you will be able to pick between many good options. Think carefully about which one of them is best for you.

IN A READING ABOUT MONEY: You have the opportunity to work toward prosperity and future wealth. Stay focused on the decision you make and don't let anything distract you.

REVERSED

You could end up having to spend more than you planned and encountering financial instability. Be ready to have to resolve some money-related issues and perhaps ask for some advice from more experienced people.

IN A READING ABOUT LOVE: Worries about money are affecting your relationship and stability. There's anxiety and tension in your life, and that's why you should plan your future with the help of your partner. Also be aware of people who might want to take advantage of you.

IN A READING ABOUT CAREER: You don't think you're doing your best and you're struggling to feel proud of what you're doing. Sometimes all it takes is a change of strategy, but you might want to consider changing careers.

IN A READING ABOUT MONEY: You haven't made a plan for your finances in a long time, and that's what's causing instability. Be careful, as you might have to pay unexpected expenses.

TWO OF PENTACLES

A young man is freely dancing, handling two golden
coins. The stormy sea and
the two ships show all the
ups and downs we can face
in life. Despite them, the
young man is able to man-
age all his problems and still
enjoy life.

TWO OF PENTACLES

STRAIGHT

There's precarity in your life, mainly focused on two
specific factors. You could be trying to keep the balance between love and work or family and health.
However, you should seek to understand why you
aren't fully stable.

IN A READING ABOUT LOVE: You're dealing
with too many responsibilities and this is affecting your romantic life. It might be necessary to
think about what your priorities are.

IN A READING ABOUT CAREER: You're
working on many different projects, and this
is making it hard for you to balance work with
personal life. Be more careful when it's time to
commit to your responsibilities.

IN A READING ABOUT MONEY: Although you're working hard, you feel like you can't be financially stable. You will find a solution soon, perhaps with a doubled source of income.

REVERSED

You're too busy, spending all your energies on different tasks, and that's why there's a lack of stability when it comes to work, money, and family. You need some time off to plan your life again.

IN A READING ABOUT LOVE: Your busy schedule is making you neglect your relationship. If you're single you might not have space in your life for a new love. Think carefully about what your priorities are.

IN A READING ABOUT CAREER: Your commitments at work are making you stressed and overwhelmed. Don't be scared to ask for help and respect your limits.

IN A READING ABOUT MONEY: It is impossible for you to save money right now. Your bills are too expensive and the only way out is to find a side project or ask for some help.

THREE OF PENTACLES

In this card we can see an apprentice who's about to do some work in a cathedral. A priest and a nobleman are discussing what changes they should make and listening to the advice of the apprentice. There is collaboration; changes are going to be made by three different forces. This card

THREE OF PENTACLES

is strictly related to work and what you can build through it.

STRAIGHT

You're enjoying expressing your creativity and all the different tasks that your work involves. Your talent is seen by people who give you recognition and admiration.

IN A READING ABOUT LOVE: You find joy and fulfilment in collaborating with your partner. You are a great team, supporting and inspiring one another. This could also mean finding love in your workplace.

IN A READING ABOUT CAREER: To succeed, you need the presence of more people.

With their help and experience and a sense of teamwork, you will accomplish great things.

IN A READING ABOUT MONEY: You're still learning how to improve your finances. Listening to others' opinions and experiences will teach you more about how to achieve wealth.

REVERSED

You don't have the support you need from your team to do a great job. Competition, bitterness, and disloyalty are a few traits that your colleagues are displaying. Expect complications to come your way.

IN A READING ABOUT LOVE: Someone in the relationship is doing all the work, while the other is not participating in everyday tasks. A lack of teamwork will cause arguments and tension.

IN A READING ABOUT CAREER: There are disputes and miscommunication within your team; competition and a lack of effort are slowing down the work. There could also be a lack of effort from your side.

IN A READING ABOUT MONEY: Everything related to money stresses you and that's why you're not interested in it at all. However, you will need to deal with your finances and learn how to manage them.

FOUR OF PENTACLES

Here we find a man far away from his home, holding a coin in his hands; he's keeping another coin on his head, while firmly holding the other two under his feet. He's so focused on holding all his coins that he can't move—he's blocked by his own possessions. This card shows avidity and attachment to money.

FOUR OF PENTACLES

STRAIGHT

You are very focused on maintaining your security regarding money and protecting everything you've achieved. While this could be a good thing, as you worked very hard to have all your possessions, being too attached to material things can easily become unhealthy.

IN A READING ABOUT LOVE: There's a heavy relationship, filled with jealousy, fear, and many other unhealthy patterns. There could also be a bond based only on money and not on passion. If you're single, you might hold on to your past too much.

IN A READING ABOUT CAREER: You've gained stability and a good position at work; however, you still fear losing everything and that's making you overly protective. Don't let your fear take over a nice moment of your life.

IN A READING ABOUT MONEY: You are able to save money to make some important investments. While this is good, remember to find the balance between being responsible and not spending money at all.

REVERSED

You have been clinging to your material possessions, avoiding changes and new experiences. Your protectiveness of your money was turning into greediness and stagnation. On the other hand, you might be spending too much money, putting yourself in difficult situations. It is time to recognize your unhealthy behaviors and commit to positive change.

IN A READING ABOUT LOVE: You're healing from unhealthy habits, giving yourself a chance to experience love without fear and jealousy.

IN A READING ABOUT CAREER: There are a couple of different interpretations. You could be using your generosity and caring attitude to help others and succeed at work, or your lack of knowledge and interest could make you lose an important position.

IN A READING ABOUT MONEY: You could be finally enjoying life and your money with family and friends, or you could be spending too much money, unaware of the damage you're creating.

FIVE OF PENTACLES

The number five is known for symbolizing adversity and that's why this card depicts a sad scene of two poor people walking in the snow, with only ragged clothes to protect them from the cold. The man is walking with crutches, while the woman tries to keep warm with an old shawl. The only source of life comes from the church's windows, where we can see the five coins.

FIVE OF PENTACLES

STRAIGHT

This card normally points to financial need and instability. You are in need of help. This could also reveal health problems and desperation. It is suggested that you consider past mistakes that could be the cause of this difficult situation.

IN A READING ABOUT LOVE: Love feels far away from you. There is loneliness, isolation, and sometimes depression in your life. A lack of financial support is affecting your romantic life as well—this applies whether you're single or not. Try to keep those you love near you.

IN A READING ABOUT CAREER: You're struggling with feeling connected with your colleagues and finding stability in your work. If you don't have the power to improve the situation, you'll have to change jobs.

IN A READING ABOUT MONEY: There's a desperate need for money as well as other materialistic resources. Don't be too proud; ask for all the help you need.

REVERSED

You're getting out of a very difficult and sad period of your life. Thanks to the people who love you, you're finding stability and peace. Now is the time to help people who are in need and struggling.

IN A READING ABOUT LOVE: After a dark time, your relationship or dating life is getting better. You're healing and feeling ready to give and receive love.

IN A READING ABOUT CAREER: The situation is not at its best, but finally there are solutions to your problems. With time and patience, everything will be fine.

IN A READING ABOUT MONEY: You're fixing all your financial problems, whether that means paying back a debt or finding a new source of income. With time you will gain more balance.

SIX OF PENTACLES

There's a wealthy man holding a scale, a symbol of fairness but also of karma. Whatever you give is what you will receive. We will find a similar message in the Magician card (see page 146). His other hand is giving money to two beggars, who are on their knees beneath him. It is a symbol

SIX OF PENTACLES

of stability and freedom to give to others without affecting your wealth.

STRAIGHT

You have a good relationship with your wealth, and you've built financial stability that gives you balance and security. You are always open to helping those in need and sharing what you possess. This could also mean that you will receive someone else's charity.

IN A READING ABOUT LOVE: Your partner is generous and supportive, and your relationship gives you inspiration and love. Remember to always find balance in love and business.

IN A READING ABOUT CAREER: Your job pays you very well, and that's why you have the chance to increase your wealth. Someone with more experience than you could help you succeed.

IN A READING ABOUT MONEY: You're in a positive situation, where you have the opportunity to work on your projects, receive the support you need, and help others.

REVERSED

This card shows an unstable relationship with money; this could mean not getting the money back from people you've helped, having big debts to pay, or acting greedily when it's time to share.

IN A READING ABOUT LOVE: There's someone in your relationship who always gives and shares, while the other one is happy only to receive. This unhealthy habit must be resolved soon.

IN A READING ABOUT CAREER: Someone around you is taking advantage of your position for their benefit. Also be careful to avoid abusing the help you're receiving.

IN A READING ABOUT MONEY: Someone could be taking advantage of you or perhaps the inverse. Another meaning is that you might not find the financial support you're seeking.

SEVEN OF PENTACLES

A young man is taking a break from his hard work to admire it. He's tired and focused on nurturing his garden so he can reap the rich results in the future. Seven is also the number of balance, universality, and mystic research. There's no space for distraction. Solitude is what is needed to think and focus.

SEVEN OF PENTACLES

STRAIGHT

Your hard work and your stable mindset are paying off. You're starting to see the results from your projects and you're learning from past mistakes. This can also show fear of losing what you have.

IN A READING ABOUT LOVE: This card signals a slow process to achieve a romantic and stable love. It could come from a friendship or it could mean you have to wait for your partner before taking the next step.

IN A READING ABOUT CAREER: You're making progress in your career, even if it's taking longer than you expected. Try to understand what you need to improve and what you have to do next.

IN A READING ABOUT MONEY: You will be able to enjoy the results you've found through your hard work and finally take a break.

REVERSED

You're not getting the results you wished for and that's why you could be feeling disappointed. Take this opportunity to set new goals and change tactics.

IN A READING ABOUT LOVE: After putting in a lot of effort, you're still not getting the romance you desire. Patience is the key as sometimes the process can take longer.

IN A READING ABOUT CAREER: You have to ask yourself if you're not working enough and getting distracted or if you're expending too much energy at work. Either way, a change of mindset is needed in order to achieve your goals.

IN A READING ABOUT MONEY: You will experience some losses, and you will not receive what you expected. A new financial plan is needed.

EIGHT OF PENTACLES

A young man is far away from people and his home, hammering a pentacle and staying focused on what he's doing. The message here is to stay completely focused on a specific task without letting distractions get in the way.

EIGHT OF PENTACLES

STRAIGHT

It's time to focus on what you want to do and dedicate all your time to work on it. This does not mean isolating yourself, but you have to be confident in achieving your goals.

IN A READING ABOUT LOVE: A stable relationship takes work, and you're willing to focus on nurturing your love. This could also indicate finding love late in life.

IN A READING ABOUT CAREER: You are focused on your job, and your commitment is bringing you rewards. You could become the leader in your team or get a promotion.

IN A READING ABOUT MONEY: Your income is increasing and that's thanks to your work. Be proud of all you're achieving.

REVERSED

You're feeling burnout from all the work you're doing. Instead of enjoying the results, you're experiencing delays, stress, and confusion. This could also suggest that the best path is taking responsibility and using your skills to improve the situation.

IN A READING ABOUT LOVE: Nothing comes without effort and love requires time and commitment. Make sure to listen to your partner's needs and invest energy in your current relationship.

IN A READING ABOUT CAREER: Although you're not content with your job, you don't feel the need to make any changes, nor to use your skills to do a good job. This could negatively affect your career.

IN A READING ABOUT MONEY: You don't want to spend time managing your finances, avoiding resolving any issue. This will have a negative impact on your stability.

NINE OF PENTACLES

A mature, wealthy woman is surrounded by vineyards, and around her we see nine pentacles. A falcon is resting in her hand, a symbol of spiritual and intellectual self-control. There is a sense of peace and fulfilment found in all the woman's achievements and success.

NINE OF PENTACLES

STRAIGHT

As the number nine brings fulfilment, you've now achieved your goals thanks to commitment, hard work, and well-earned skills. You should enjoy everything you've worked for and feel proud of yourself.

IN A READING ABOUT LOVE: Whether you're in a relationship or not, you're feeling pleased with your life and enjoying what you possess. This makes you attractive to others and nice to be around.

IN A READING ABOUT CAREER: You have abundance and prosperity around you, whether it is from a job or your business. Enjoy every achievement you've accomplished.

IN A READING ABOUT MONEY: You have everything you need, as well as money and stability. If you want to make a big investment, this is the right time.

REVERSED

You could be experiencing some financial loss or perhaps you're financially depending on someone else. This could also show the inability to relax after years of hard work. Either way, you should take a step back and resolve the situation.

IN A READING ABOUT LOVE: Something is bothering you regarding your romantic life and it's making you feel insecure. Be open about how you're feeling and what you need.

IN A READING ABOUT CAREER: You've worked hard and still feel like you're not gaining anything, or all you want is success, but you don't want to make any effort. This card also suggests that you watch out for dishonest colleagues.

IN A READING ABOUT MONEY: This card can show you that your actions could lead to bankruptcy if you engage in irresponsible spending, or if you're dependent on someone else.

TEN OF PENTACLES

An old man is surrounded by his family and dogs just outside his city. He looks to be the head of the family, finally resting and enjoying the fruits of a life of hard work. He's able to provide stability to his family while retaining harmony, grati- tude, and prosperity.

TEN OF PENTACLES

STRAIGHT

Everything you've worked for will pay off, giving you long-term stability and security. You can now relax and be happy and satisfied with what you've built.

IN A READING ABOUT LOVE: You and your partner are building a strong relationship and you could be feeling ready to move in together or start a family. If you're single, you will find someone with values you share who is ready for a serious relationship.

IN A READING ABOUT CAREER: Your work will provide you long-term stability and income. You will provide your family with wealth and security.

IN A READING ABOUT MONEY: This card
is a sign of good luck. You might receive an
unexpected donation or be able to save for your
future and retirement.

REVERSED

A sudden problem will occur, whether it is a
financial loss or an issue with a family member.
Temporary stability can achieved if you give the
problem enough attention.

IN A READING ABOUT LOVE: You are too
concerned about what your family might think
of your partner, or there could be arguments
between your partner and a family member.
Remember to always maintain your boundaries.

IN A READING ABOUT CAREER: Your job
and business are unstable, which could lead you
to be jobless. You'd better find a plan B.

IN A READING ABOUT MONEY: You could
be having big family arguments about money
or lose a huge amount of money. Be careful and
ready to resolve important issues.

THE SUIT OF SWORDS

STRAIGHT: Intelligence, communication

REVERSED: Aggression, confusion

ELEMENT: Air

ASTROLOGY: Gemini, Libra, Aquarius

The Suit of Swords represents the qualities of logic and communication, how we relate to people, and how we manage conflicts. It brings us knowledge and it shows how we think; the cards can also be referred to as cards of arrows, knives, sabers, or daggers, and they are often associated with pain caused by challenging moments and overthinking.

As the element is air, we will engage in everything that involves our rational mind, intelligence, and discipline. When reversed, we can see aggression, confusion, and coldness in how we behave.

KING OF SWORDS

The King is sitting on his throne and holding his sword upright, giving a sense of authority, responsibility, and clear thinking. The purple tunic shows spiritual understanding; the butterfly shows transformation; the sky is clear at the top but cloudy at the bottom, which shows that his rigidity could have negative effects.

KING OF SWORDS

STRAIGHT

The best thing you can do is use all your logic and focus to find the truth and stick to it. Try to have a clear understanding of the situation, using all your rationality.

IN A READING ABOUT LOVE: More than romance, this card brings mutual respect, intelligence, and reliability. You and your partner are doing your best to have a good life. If you're single, keep your standards high.

IN A READING ABOUT CAREER: You always want to show the world your best, constantly pushing your abilities further. This is what will make you succeed in your career.

IN A READING ABOUT MONEY: Always look at your finances with logic; do your due diligence before making any decision.

REVERSED

Sometimes being authoritative and strict can have negative repercussions. You might be sharp in the way you talk and selfish in what you expect. This could also mean you have problems managing anger.

IN A READING ABOUT LOVE: This shows a person who's manipulative and selfish in their actions. There are uncontrolled emotions that are ruining the relationship. If you're single, it could mean your standards are too low.

IN A READING ABOUT CAREER: There is aggressiveness, attachment to power, and control and disrespect. If this doesn't reflect a colleague, it could mean you should analyze your own behavior.

IN A READING ABOUT MONEY: You have been very careless in your spending and now you're trying to fix the situation with pointless loopholes.

QUEEN OF SWORDS

The Queen is sitting on her throne, looking firm and introspective. She points upward with her sword, showing her ability to always see the truth, as no one can lie or trick her. The bird in the sky is another symbol that shows her ability to go beyond any obstacle to find a solution.

QUEEN OF SWORDS

STRAIGHT

You have to make decisions based on your judgment and not only on your emotions. Just as the Queen extends her hand, you should always have compassion but never avoid telling the truth.

IN A READING ABOUT LOVE: You can be solitary and your intellect can make you very selective. As you value independence, it might be difficult for others to get closer to you romantically.

IN A READING ABOUT CAREER: You are wise, respectful, and good at what you do. People respect you and your wisdom; communication is your dominant skill.

IN A READING ABOUT MONEY: Make sure you have a balance between emotions and logic. Respect your boundaries and don't go past your limits.

REVERSED

You're basing your decisions solely on your emotions without using rationality. Being too emotional is preventing you from finding clarity. You might also have become bitter and coldhearted in relation to others.

IN A READING ABOUT LOVE: You or your partner are being overly judgmental and manipulative. These behaviors are best resolved in therapy with the help of a professional. If you're single, this could reveal the pain you're experiencing after a breakup.

IN A READING ABOUT CAREER: There's someone who is nasty in the way they communicate and perhaps has repressed anger. Whether this is you or a colleague, it is best to not let it ruin the work environment and your stability.

IN A READING ABOUT MONEY: Your lack of good communication has put you in a bad position financially. Make sure to work on the way you communicate when it comes to your money.

KNIGHT OF SWORDS

The young man is decisively riding his horse through a turbulent environment. He's not scared of what is coming and he's guided by his intellectual energy, symbolized by the white horse.

KNIGHT OF SWORDS

STRAIGHT

You're very passionate about your goals and dreams and your active mind is making you very determined. However, without compassion and balance, your drive to manifest your goals can turn into negativity and carelessness.

IN A READING ABOUT LOVE: You struggle to emotionally connect with someone else and commit to a long-term relationship, as you need to be mentally stimulated. This could also mean you need to be more courageous when it comes to love.

IN A READING ABOUT CAREER: You know what you want and you know how to get it. This confidence often scares people, but it shouldn't stop you from taking big steps.

IN A READING ABOUT MONEY: Keep being committed and focused and you'll be able to strengthen your financial stability.

REVERSED

There are uncontrolled emotions, impulsiveness, and a lack of patience when it comes to working hard to accomplish something. The lack of organization should be a red flag and inspiration to do a lot of inner work.

IN A READING ABOUT LOVE: Arguments and dishonesty are weakening your relationship. There's manipulation and aggressiveness to the point where you should consider ending the relationship.

IN A READING ABOUT CAREER: Despite hurting others through your manner of communicating, you are willing to use your arrogance as a skill to succeed. You might want to reconsider your tactic and language.

IN A READING ABOUT MONEY: You or someone close to you is so obsessed with money that they are not paying attention to how it can impact people. A balance is needed between material things and emotions.

PAGE OF SWORDS

A young man is holding his sword with both hands. The wind blows in the trees and the terrain is uneven. His energy and temperament make clear how secure he is in himself; however, this could be either positive or negative.

PAGE OF SWORDS

STRAIGHT

You're a curious person, always keen to learn and discover information; you're energetic and passionate about your dreams. You might want to manage your high energy, as it might seem almost too much to others. This card suggests talking, opening up, and expressing your ideas to others and taking their advice into consideration.

IN A READING ABOUT LOVE: Someone feels like their emotions are not being taken seriously and small things are always turning into arguments. You must handle emotions properly to avoid a breakup.

IN A READING ABOUT CAREER: You have a lot of energy and motivation to succeed in your career. Stay dedicated and you'll be able to take big steps forward.

IN A READING ABOUT MONEY: You have a lot of ideas, but you still need to learn more from experienced people. Take some time to learn more about how to manage your money.

REVERSED

All the positive traits of this card turn into negative ones. An active mind and drive for success are becoming dangerous and hurtful to people. There could be empty lies and irrational behaviors.

IN A READING ABOUT LOVE: Insensitivity and inability to communicate are the main characteristics found here when it comes to love. More flexibility and empathy are needed to make the relationship work.

IN A READING ABOUT CAREER: You have a lot of ideas, but without channeling your energies in one direction you won't be able to move forward. Take some time to find more clarity.

IN A READING ABOUT MONEY: You're spending a lot of time planning without actually going anywhere. More practicality is required.

ACE OF SWORDS

The size of the sword represents masculine forces, and is a symbol of strength and power in relation to justice and morals. There has been a victory after a long battle. This card is characterized by honesty and fairness.

ACE OF SWORDS

STRAIGHT

You're seeing the world with eyes of truth, justice, and honesty. There is no deception, and you're in the perfect mindset to work toward what you want. Use these qualities correctly, as they could turn into unhealthy behavior.

IN A READING ABOUT LOVE: Intellectual conversations and talking about problems are healthy habits that you and your partner have. Always try to be open and honest about how you feel. This can also be an encouragement to leave toxic people out of your life.

IN A READING ABOUT CAREER: This card brings new projects, opportunities, and perhaps a new job. You enjoy communicating with your colleagues and setting new goals.

IN A READING ABOUT MONEY: You'll be presented with an important decision to make. Make sure you don't listen only to your heart—use rationality and logic.

REVERSED

There is a strong destructive behavior characterized by anger, aggressiveness, and manipulation. This could be caused by traumas or difficult events. However, some work has to be done to manage these emotions.

IN A READING ABOUT LOVE: Difficult arguments and miscommunication are causing pain in your relationship. Make sure to pay attention to improving communication.

IN A READING ABOUT CAREER: Your ideas might not turn out how you expected; be ready for some disappointments and miscommunication with your colleagues.

IN A READING ABOUT MONEY: You don't have a clear view of your finances. Try to always keep track of your situation to avoid unpleasant surprises.

TWO OF SWORDS

A blindfolded woman is sitting near the sea, holding two crossed swords. The rocky sea is a representation of the problems we can encounter in life. The band over her eyes stops her from having clear vision, making it hard for her to make decisions. The two swords represent the balance between intellect and logic. The crescent moon shows deception, but also how she should trust her intuition.

TWO OF SWORDS

STRAIGHT

You will soon be in a situation where you'll have to make an important decision. Two forces are battling against each other, putting you in a difficult position. Act with caution and take some time to think and listen to your intuition.

IN A READING ABOUT LOVE: If you're single you might feel stuck, unable to move forward. If you're in a relationship there could be problems that you and your partner can't resolve. Never avoid making important decisions.

IN A READING ABOUT CAREER: You have two options to choose between, whether you have to pick between jobs or two people. Take some time to think carefully about what is best.

IN A READING ABOUT MONEY: You're trying to avoid facing your finances, risking spending more than you can afford. Be careful to avoid creating more debts.

REVERSED

You're surrounded by lies and deception, and people around you are not being fully honest with you. You could also feel the pressure to make a decision you don't want to make.

IN A READING ABOUT LOVE: You have to make a choice that is causing you pain and confusion. It is better to make the decision now than to wait longer.

IN A READING ABOUT CAREER: You have to make important decisions, or perhaps you're between two colleagues fighting and you don't know what to do. There will be confusion and indecision regarding what the best move is.

IN A READING ABOUT MONEY: You're trying to improve your finances but that's making you stressed and overwhelmed. Give it time and you'll sort everything out.

THREE OF SWORDS

This is probably one of the most famous Minor Arcana; a heart, a symbol of warmth and love, is pierced by three swords against a rainy background. This card reveals pain, grief, and loss. The dreary background can be a representation of the moment you're in now.

THREE OF SWORDS

STRAIGHT

This card warns of betrayal, pain, heartbreak, and rejection. Although these are all hard emotions to embrace, they are part of life. Seeing the situation as impermanent can help relieve the pain.

IN A READING ABOUT LOVE: There are tears and pain in your life right now. Whether your partner is creating trouble or someone else is, there are major problems to be solved. Always put your happiness first.

IN A READING ABOUT CAREER: Your workplace is stressful and affects your mood in a negative way, or you could be risking losing your job. You have the power to get through this difficult situation.

IN A READING ABOUT MONEY: You went through a big loss that is affecting your financial stability. Give yourself time to sort everything out.

REVERSED

You're just coming out of a difficult and painful moment in your life. Although it's over, you're still dealing with the pain. As you deal with it, remember there are happy and joyful moments awaiting you.

IN A READING ABOUT LOVE: You're healing from past traumas and ready to forgive. Whether you're still in a relationship or not, remember not to repress your feelings, and move on.

IN A READING ABOUT CAREER: You're slowly solving all the stressful issues you had at work. This could also mean that someone is being negative and holding grudges against you.

IN A READING ABOUT MONEY: You're rebuilding your stability, and although it will take time, you will be able to create security and find the balance between spending and saving.

FOUR OF SWORDS

A knight is lying down in a tomb in a church. His hands are in a praying position. Three swords hang above him and one lies beneath. The three hanging swords show the suffering the man has gone through in life, and the sword beneath him shows it is time to rest, as the battle is now over.

FOUR OF SWORDS

STRAIGHT

It is time to retreat. Take time for yourself to rest, think, and take care of your body and mind. Although we might think this card brings vulnerability, it brings strength and clarity instead. However, a moment of peace and calm is needed before taking action.

IN A READING ABOUT LOVE: You could be feeling tired and emotionally drained right now. If you're single, take a break from dating and give yourself time to recharge. If you're in a relationship, it is the moment to take some time off with your partner, perhaps on a vacation.

IN A READING ABOUT CAREER: You need some time to take care of yourself, as work has been too stressful and frustrating.

IN A READING ABOUT MONEY: You need some time off without thinking about money and how to make more. Take some time on your own where money is not involved.

REVERSED

Even if you need some rest, you're unable to take time off, as you always feel like you can't stop. Allowing yourself a break might be necessary.

IN A READING ABOUT LOVE: Rather than taking a break from your lover, this suggests spending time on your own or enjoying some time together after a period of calmness.

IN A READING ABOUT CAREER: You need to learn how to listen to your body and mind. Don't be afraid to act when you need to rest and recharge your battery.

IN A READING ABOUT MONEY: You're feeling like you can't manage your finances alone, and that's why seeking help from an expert might be a good idea.

FIVE OF SWORDS

A young man has won over his enemies, and with a content look, he holds their swords. Although the battle seems over, the cloudy sky is telling us that it's not, despite what the young man thinks.

FIVE OF SWORDS

STRAIGHT

You will engage in some sort of conflict with family or friends. Instead of trying to understand and find a compromise, your arrogance will worsen the situation.

IN A READING ABOUT LOVE: There's tension in the air, and some arguments are about to take place. Make sure your ego does not make you act in an immature way.

IN A READING ABOUT CAREER: There are conflicts and nasty arguments in your workplace and you will be involved somehow. Remember to act professionally; do not let arrogance take over.

IN A READING ABOUT MONEY: There will be arguments involving money with someone close to you. This card also suggests improving your savings techniques.

REVERSED

Despite the stressful arguments you're facing, you are slowly understanding that forgiveness is better than trying to always be right. There is no space for egotistical behavior and resentment.

IN A READING ABOUT LOVE: You need to find your peace, whether this means finding a solution with your partner or leaving the relationship. Make sure you don't act based on pure anger.

IN A READING ABOUT CAREER: A slow, positive change is happening at your workplace, and many disputes seem to be over. This could also mean the opposite and there could be a worsening of the situation.

IN A READING ABOUT MONEY: Stay away from people who only care about your finances; take this moment to relax and avoid letting money stress you.

SIX OF SWORDS

A man is paddling a boat with a woman and child on board. There's a message of change and leaving something behind. The woman, who doesn't show her face, seems sad; this could also represent grief and leaving something painful behind.

SIX OF SWORDS

STRAIGHT

You're experiencing a transition that is not easy and is perhaps leaving you with sadness. Despite the pain, you know that this change is necessary.

IN A READING ABOUT LOVE: This can mean ending a relationship or closing a painful chapter and starting over with your partner. This can also signal that you're ready for new love after a period of pain.

IN A READING ABOUT CAREER: Recent changes have resulted in your ability to leave stress behind. Now you can relax and benefit from this new chapter.

IN A READING ABOUT MONEY: You can now take a breath and leave all the struggles of the past behind. However, the future is still coming; remember that financial issues should be avoided.

REVERSED

You're trying to move on but you're struggling to let go of your past. On the other hand, this could indicate you don't want to make changes that need to be made.

IN A READING ABOUT LOVE: You are struggling to let go of something from your past that is making you insecure and unstable. If you're with someone toxic and careless, it is best to move on and start a new chapter.

IN A READING ABOUT CAREER: Despite your attempts, work always seems to bring troubles and stress. You might want to take a look at your behavior and consider if you're perhaps being too defensive.

IN A READING ABOUT MONEY: You're trying to avoid issues related to your money, but these will only get bigger if you don't try to solve them.

SEVEN OF SWORDS

Here there's a man who's walking away with four swords, while the other three are still stuck in the ground. We can see that he's quite pleased with himself for stealing the swords, but he doesn't realize that far away a group of soldiers has found out what he's doing.

SEVEN OF SWORDS

STRAIGHT

You or someone else is being dishonest and trying to escape from the consequences of their bad actions. There's betrayal in this card and an unwillingness to take responsibility. This could also reveal the need to be alone for some time.

IN A READING ABOUT LOVE: There are many lies that have been told and someone is trying to avoid facing them. It is time to take action and find the truth.

IN A READING ABOUT CAREER: This could mean someone in your workplace is sneaking around behind your back or that you need a better strategy to showcase your skills.

IN A READING ABOUT MONEY: There could be scammers or people close to you who are trying to trick you and take your money. Keep an eye out and don't lose your money.

REVERSED

There's a change in someone's behavior, because after many lies and unhealthy behaviors, they are now choosing to tell the truth. Although this can be difficult, it is always better to promote honesty.

IN A READING ABOUT LOVE: You will get to the bottom of some complicated situations where many lies were told. With the anxiety that this could have caused, you will at least feel freed from the burden.

IN A READING ABOUT CAREER: Someone is being exposed at work after being complicit in a dishonest situation. This could bring justice or escalate the situation and cause more drama.

IN A READING ABOUT MONEY: You haven't been fully honest in dealing with your money and you'll probably need to face the consequences soon.

EIGHT OF SWORDS

EIGHT OF SWORDS

This dark representation shows a woman tied up and blindfolded, surrounded by a fence of eight swords. In this card, there's a sense of desolation and having nowhere to run.

STRAIGHT

You feel like you're trapped, stuck in a situation without a solution. This feeling is caused by your behaviors and past choices and now it feels like it's too late to do anything. It is advised that you try to look at the situation for what it is; find a solution using logic and take responsibility.

IN A READING ABOUT LOVE: You're feeling trapped in a relationship, or if you're single, you might be acting passively. It is your responsibility to change your behavior and your life.

IN A READING ABOUT CAREER: You're not happy with your professional situation and you feel like you need to change paths. This is difficult and could cause anxiety. Seek help and advice and you'll find a solution.

IN A READING ABOUT MONEY: Your financial situation is giving you anxiety and a sense of discouragement. However, you have the skills and tools to improve it. It is time to take some action!

REVERSED

You're aware of your past mistakes and you're ready to change habits that weren't helping you feel happy. You should be proud of your self-improvements and willingness to change.

IN A READING ABOUT LOVE: Your needs and the way you see life are changing and that's why you're seeing love with different eyes. You now know what you need to feel happy and fulfilled.

IN A READING ABOUT CAREER: You are more aware of your skills and you know what moves to make next in order to succeed. This card could also show a lack of hope and excitement for the future.

IN A READING ABOUT MONEY: Your fear in relation to money is either gone or increased. If you still feel anxious about your financial situation, you should try to understand the root of the problem and then solve it.

NINE OF SWORDS

In this card there is a sense of despair and anxiety. A woman who just woke up from a nightmare seems upset and scared. Although she has protection in the form of the nine swords hanging on her wall, she can't escape her pain, as it comes from inside.

NINE OF SWORDS

STRAIGHT

Something painful is haunting you, keeping you up at night. This could perhaps be a trauma that you cannot deal with on your own. What we discovered in Eight of Swords is now plaguing your mind, creating confusion and intrusive thoughts.

IN A READING ABOUT LOVE: A painful situation is causing you anxiety, remorse, and fear. You're avoiding getting to the root of the problems because you're scared of their nature. If you're single, a past relationship might be haunting you.

IN A READING ABOUT CAREER: Other than signaling severe anxiety and stress at your workplace, this card could also indicate a possible paranoia. Perhaps things are not as bad as you think; if you can't manage the stress though, changing jobs or seeking professional help are valid options.

IN A READING ABOUT MONEY: You're going through a stressful period financially, but you are also making the issue seem bigger than it is. Try to look at problems with rationality and you'll find a solution.

REVERSED

The meaning of the reversed card is very similar to the upright version. There's a trauma or painful experience that is coming back to your mind, causing anxiety and fear. However, now you have hope and the understanding that this pain will not last forever if you work through it.

IN A READING ABOUT LOVE: You're ready to face your pain and traumas and put an end to your fears. Through inner work and open discussions, you will be able to start a new chapter.

IN A READING ABOUT CAREER: The problems at work could ease or get worse; you now know that everything will come to an end, and thanks to your new mindset, you will be able to get through the situation without experiencing anxiety.

IN A READING ABOUT MONEY: Depending on what cards are next to this one, your financial state could improve or get much more complicated. If the latter scenario is the case, seek external help from professionals.

TEN OF SWORDS

The terrifying scene in this card depicts a dead man stabbed by ten swords. He's lying down on the ground with a cloth covering him from his chest to his feet. The dark, cloudy sky and standing water represent stillness and negativity. Despite the enormous pain in this card, the sun is still rising in the distance.

TEN OF SWORDS

STRAIGHT

You're probably at a low point in life. There's betrayal and suffering in your life. The swords symbolize logic and intellect and that's what is stabbing you. The pain is not external but part of you. You are able to get rid of this pain and start a new chapter.

IN A READING ABOUT LOVE: This card often reveals an imminent breakup or end of a relationship. Sometimes it indicates betrayal and infidelity. Although there's a lot of pain right now, you will find happiness again within.

IN A READING ABOUT CAREER: Colleagues at work might be unbearable right now. Work might be stressful and draining, and sometimes this indicates the end of a job. Take this moment as an opportunity to grow.

IN A READING ABOUT MONEY: Your investments are not paying off and you should make sure you have some savings. Avoid making risky movements.

REVERSED

The reversed card still brings suffering and sorrow, but you're aware that it can't get worse. You know you can get through this period and that from now on it can only get better.

IN A READING ABOUT LOVE: You're slowly healing from past wounds and emotional traumas. Although it is not easy, you're acknowledging the work you need to do and you'll soon recover.

IN A READING ABOUT CAREER: You're slowly getting out of a stressful situation; whether you changed jobs or managed to resolve some issue, work is far less stressful and disruptive now.

IN A READING ABOUT MONEY: You're getting out of an extremely tough situation where you almost went bankrupt. May this be a lesson so that you won't repeat the same mistakes.

CHAPTER
THREE

MAJOR
ARCANA

THE MAJOR ARCANA are 22 cards with a deep and profound meaning that represent the foundation of human nature and awareness. They reveal karmic influences and lessons that impact your life, as well as your unique path as a magickal being working toward enlightenment.

THE FOOL: 0

STRAIGHT: New beginnings, freedom

REVERSED: Inconsideration, stagnation

ELEMENT: Air

ASTROLOGY: Uranus

The Fool is the first card of the Major Arcana, considered the first and the last of the deck. It represents a young man starting a journey, without a precise destination but on the way to gaining wisdom. It shows someone who is a relatively naive, free, and faithful person ready to embark on a

THE FOOL

new adventure, unaware of any danger and ready to follow their beliefs to find the truth.

In some representations we can find a young man without many belongings at the edge of a cliff, looking content. This can represent being open to new roads in life without needing to possess many material items. In other representations, we can find a young man with an animal, often a dog. Here, the animal represents our natural instinct.

This card can then represent the imminent start of a new path in life, a difficult challenge that has the potential to be overcome, or the arrival of something or someone new.

The Fool can be crazy, unpredictable, joyful, and amazed; when it's the first card to appear during a reading, it is a good sign and it lowers the intensity of other possible "negative" messages that other cards can bring.

STRAIGHT:

The Fool means you're ready to start a new chapter of your life where you can feel free to follow your heart. Embrace your faith and be open to new experiences; this will make you grow and mature as a person. See every day as an adventure, let your inner child guide you, and enjoy a simple life with no worries and no expectation of what is coming next.

IN A READING ABOUT LOVE: This means you need to be open to new experiences in order to encounter a new love. Don't be afraid of exploring and expanding your vision: Something new is coming your way. If you're in a relationship, it means it is time to move on to a new chapter with your love, enjoying freedom and positivity.

IN READING ABOUT CAREER: This card is encouraging you, especially if you were thinking of changing jobs, asking for a promotion, or making drastic changes in your career. You'll have new ideas and the chance to learn a lot. Have the courage to start new projects and take risks.

IN A READING ABOUT MONEY: Pay attention and don't be too naive when it comes to your money. It is a good moment to start a new business. Remember to follow your intuition and you'll feel like you have everything you always needed.

REVERSED

When the Fool is reversed, it shows signs of apathy, imprudence, and inconsistency, which often bring negative results. You might feel like it is not the right time to act; you might have a sense of lethargy. It can indicate that you're not aware of the negative repercussions of your actions and that you are not planning for your future. This card is a reminder to consider every side of the situation you're in and to be careful before making a decision.

IN A READING ABOUT LOVE: Think carefully about who is in front of you, as appearances might hide the true selves of others. It can show how you or your partner are currently too immature to stay in the relationship, or indicate that a relationship might end and give you more freedom as a result.

IN A READING ABOUT CAREER: You might feel stuck in your current job, like you're not getting anything out of your career. Think carefully about how your actions might affect your colleagues or yourself before taking them. Don't rush to change jobs—take the time to think about all possibilities.

IN A READING ABOUT MONEY: This might indicate that you are being careless about your spending or not fully aware of your current financial situation. Someone might take advantage of your lack of attention or you might find yourself in a tricky situation. Always keep your guard up.

THE MAGICIAN: 1

STRAIGHT: Manifestation, willpower

REVERSED: Deception, illusions

ELEMENT: Air

ASTROLOGY: Mercury

The Magician card is full of symbolism; in the Marseilles Deck, you might confuse it for the Juggler, as his appearance doesn't look like a traditional magician's. In the Rider-Waite-Smith deck, we can see a man behind a table, in a lovely garden full of roses and lilies. His clothes are white, which symbolizes willingness.

THE MAGICIAN

With one hand holding a wand pointing upward, he's connecting to the divine energy coming from above; with the other hand, he's pointing downward, sending the divine energy below him as a way to show that he is freely giving it. This, especially for witches, can remind us of the saying "as above, so below." Although it is a very complicated phrase, it essentially means that the earth is a reflection of what's above, and what's outside is a reflection of what's within. The Magician channels energy between the above and below worlds.

On the table, we find the signs of the Minor Arcana: wands, cups, pentacles, and swords, representing the four elements. This card symbolizes the ability to work with occult forces and the universe.

The Magician can manipulate the energies of the spiritual and material world, allowing him to obtain what he desires. It reveals that the person who got this card has incredible powers, even if they're not aware of it.

The infinity sign above his head symbolizes that what we are inside is what we manifest outside; every single action we take, even when it appears meaningless, it is connected to something bigger.

STRAIGHT

The Magician suggests that we be more aware of how the spiritual and material worlds are connected, of how magick and spirituality are vital for our existence on earth. The snake around the Magician's hips symbolizes change. It is the right time to make important decisions and listen to our inner voice. The time to act is now, so use your power to create the life you always wanted.

IN A READING ABOUT LOVE: For both single people and those in relationships, this card brings excitement, love, and the power to create the life you want. Enjoy your spiritual journey with your partner and keep inspiring and motivating one another.

IN A READING ABOUT CAREER: You have the drive to succeed. You just need to set your goal and manifest it. You have the ability to turn your career into something extraordinary. This card can also mean the presence of a new colleague or investor—choose the people who will accompany you in your career carefully.

IN A READING ABOUT MONEY: It is time to take control over your financial situation. Tap into your ability to attract wealth and abundance. Use all the tools you have to increase your income and enjoy the results of your work.

REVERSED

You might feel disconnected from the world, anxious, down, and like you are struggling with communication. You are not aligned with your self-confidence. In fact, this card reversed might show that it is not the right time to take action. You need to take time to develop your powers and connect with your spiritual self. The Magician reversed could also show the presence of someone who is not being truthful, who is manipulating you for their own interests.

IN A READING ABOUT LOVE: You or your partner are engaging in unhealthy behaviors and one of you might be keeping secrets. If you're starting a new relationship, make sure to get to know your lover as best you can; sometimes what seems like reality is only an illusion.

IN A READING ABOUT CAREER: You might not be realizing your full potential, letting fear hold you back. Think carefully, when taking risks, about the potential consequences. Be wary that someone at work might not be completely sincere.

IN A READING ABOUT MONEY: Your financial situation is not what you want it to be; this might be because you're not connected to your full potential and skills. Boost your self-confidence and always be aware of those who could mislead you.

THE HIGH PRIESTESS: 2

STRAIGHT: Intuition, inner voice

REVERSED: Unawareness, repressed feelings

ELEMENT: Water

ASTROLOGY: Moon

The High Priestess can be considered almost the opposite of our previous card, the Magician. If with the Magician we were embracing masculine energy, actively working with energies, and dominating reality, with the High Priestess, we welcome feminine energy, intuition,

THE HIGH PRIESTESS

devotion, meditation, and the subconscious.

We see her represented sitting on a square stone between two pillars at Solomon's Temple. The pillar on the left has the letter "B," which stands for Boaz and symbolizes strength; the pillar on the right has the letter "J," which stands for Jachin and symbolizes establishment. The two pillars also represent duality—duality between good and evil, positive and negative, masculine and feminine.

The High Priestess is holding and protecting a scroll, which is a sign that she is not sharing all her knowledge, but is keeping her secrets. She wears the crown of Isis, which could show she believes in magick. The crescent moon is a symbol we find associated with Saint Mary in many representations, and it means she has control over her emotions.

The High Priestess, as her number also suggests, represents duality in its fullest meaning. With this card, dive deeper into hidden meaning, abandoning shallowness.

STRAIGHT

When the High Priestess appears straight in a reading, it suggests that you should closely monitor your intuition and dreams in order to listen to your inner voice. It's not time to act or make quick decisions; bring calm and introspection into your life, and spend some time on your own without being affected by anxiety, fear, and impatience. The answers to your questions come from within—use meditation and prayers to find out more.

IN A READING ABOUT LOVE: It can indicate that underneath calm emotions there is a fiery passion. If you are in a relationship, there will be a deep romance and powerful feelings between you and your partner—always remember to be grounded in reality. If you're looking for love, always be honest with yourself and others.

IN A READING ABOUT CAREER: Rely on your instincts when it's time to make important decisions. New ideas might come to you and there's also the chance that this is a good time to return to school. In addition to the development of creativity, this card can also suggest the study of spirituality, psychology, or other healing practices.

IN A READING ABOUT MONEY: Do not overshare about your financial situation. Pay attention to how much money you spend and always listen to your gut before making an important decision.

REVERSED

The High Priestess reversed indicates that you're not in tune with your intuition. You're struggling to feel connected with your inner self and are asking yourself questions about your life. This is a call for you to welcome spirituality into your life. You are fearing others' opinions and hiding your true self. You might encounter issues with health, confusion, and some changes in your job. The way to get rid of this imbalanced situation is to explore your spiritual self.

IN A READING ABOUT LOVE: You might be experiencing a period of isolation that is holding you back from making deep connections. Always be true to your feelings and never avoid telling the truth to others.

IN A READING ABOUT CAREER: Your lack of intuition is making you feel discontent and disconnected from your job. Learn how to listen to your inner voice, and be wary that there might be a colleague who does not have your back.

IN A READING ABOUT MONEY: Do not rely on other people to sort out your financial situation. You're not aware of details and small problems related to money. Use meditation to increase your awareness.

THE EMPRESS: 3

STRAIGHT: Fertility, feminine power

REVERSED: Dependence, low self-esteem

ELEMENT: Earth

ASTROLOGY: Venus

The Empress, as we can see from the cushion she's sitting on, is connected to Venus. It represents the feminine power in the material world, as opposed to the High Priestess, which is connected to the spiritual one.

THE EMPRESS

It brings fertility, harmony, beauty, and luxury; we can see a mature woman wearing a dress with pomegranates on it, which symbolize fertility, and holding a scepter, which represents the world.

The stars on her head represent the zodiac signs and the connection with higher realms. The flourishing nature that surrounds her brings abundance and a deep connection with nature and the desire to reproduce.

STRAIGHT

The Empress embodies feminine power in its every sense; it relates to expression, creativity, happiness, pregnancy, and motherhood. When a pregnancy is not involved, it can also indicate caring behavior and a sense of motherhood. It is the birth of new ideas, projects, and good luck. It suggests spending more time in nature and developing self-love.

IN A READING ABOUT LOVE: This indicates a loving relationship based on respect and mature decisions. It can also predict pregnancy or a wedding.

IN A READING ABOUT CAREER: You're putting a lot of work into creating a harmonious environment; you're full of new ideas and fully committed to your job. You feel in sync with what you're doing and enjoy your workplace. It can also show the presence of a kind and caring colleague.

IN A READING ABOUT MONEY: You will find good luck and abundance in your future financial situation. You will soon experience financial stability and be generous with friends and family.

REVERSED:

You might have spent too much time caring for others, forgetting to nurture yourself with love and attention. You might feel exhausted and too tired to try to balance every aspect of your life. Find the strength that is within you and do not rely on others to take care of you.

IN A READING ABOUT LOVE: You need to find more balance between what you need and what your partner needs; your self-worth is too low and this will affect your relationship or a future one. This card can also show infidelity or reduced interest in sex.

IN A READING ABOUT CAREER: You may have taken on too many responsibilities or perhaps you feel like you don't have enough energy to do your best. Colleagues at work might not appreciate your work and you could feel disconnected with your skills. It's time to sort out these problems, whether this means developing more confidence or changing jobs.

IN A READING ABOUT MONEY: This card does not show a lack of money, but instead a lack of stability and self-belief. You need to understand what is making you feel unstable and protect what's yours.

THE EMPEROR: 4

STRAIGHT: Control, masculine power

REVERSED: Tyranny, lack of self-confidence

ELEMENT: Fire

ASTROLOGY: Aries

The Emperor, as the name suggests, gives us a sense of authority and command. We see a mature, strong man sitting on a throne made out of stone with the heads of four rams sculpted into it, which signifies the zodiac sign Aries. The next twelve cards will be associated with the zodiac signs.

THE EMPEROR

Aries is the first of them and represents ambition related to command and power. The long beard is a sign of experience, while the mountains behind him show his sense of leadership. His armor shows he's ready for conflicts but also serves to protect, while his tunic is connected to Mars and Aries.

In fact, while the Empress is a mother figure, the Emperor represents a father.

STRAIGHT

This card represents a paternal figure that embodies order, organization, structure, and strategic thinking. Although he is a strong authority and presence, the Emperor always wants the best for everyone and is not a tyrannical personality. It might indicate your need to step forward and make important decisions in your life, or it can also be related to your relationship with your father.

IN A READING ABOUT LOVE: This card does not represent romance but it is not necessarily a bad card. It shows stability and maturity and focuses on material matters, such as money or common sense. It can also show the presence of an older figure who struggles to express their feelings.

IN A READING ABOUT CAREER: This card encourages you to be persistent and continue your hard work even during hard times. It brings organization, confidence, and leadership.

IN A READING ABOUT MONEY: You need to focus more on how you spend your money. Track all the money that goes in and out of your bank account; by doing so you will guarantee financial stability and success.

REVERSED

The Emperor reversed can reveal immaturity, lack of ambition, and conflict with authority figures. Someone might be abusing his power—it could be your father or partner. It can also mean you are in a weak position, trying to avoid any responsibilities. On a more personal side, this card reversed can indicate your lack of self-control and an absence of structure in your life.

IN A READING ABOUT LOVE: Someone in the relationship is the leader, making all the decisions and dictating them to the other. It can also indicate a struggle to connect emotionally in your relationship (or budding relationship), a lack of communication, and infertility.

IN A READING ABOUT CAREER: You might be experiencing a lack of attention and commitment in your job, and this could lead you to feel unsatisfied. It can also show a tyrannical presence in your work environment. If this is the case, find a new job.

IN A READING ABOUT MONEY: You have to overcome your lack of self-confidence if you want to improve financially. You have to learn how to manage and spend your money—this will prevent unpleasant situations.

THE HIEROPHANT: 5

STRAIGHT: Spiritual authority, conformity

REVERSED: New beliefs, rebellion

ELEMENT: Earth

ASTROLOGY: Taurus

The Hierophant (or the Pope, the High Priest) is a highly powerful figure, a spiritual authority. As we can see in this representation, two monks are listening to him, wearing clothes with roses that symbolize divine love and lilies that symbolize purity (we see the same symbols in the Magician card).

THE HIEROPHANT

The Hierophant is wearing an elaborate vest that symbolizes the three worlds. We can see many sacred symbols repeated three times: The three crosses on his white band, the crown with its three layers, the triple cross in his left hand, and three fingers raised in his right hand. All this symbolizes the principle of connection between chorus, soul, and spirit.

In particular, the three crosses on his white band represent the Father, Son, and Holy Ghost, and his right hand is raised in an act of benediction. The two keys beneath indicate the power that conformity and tradition have in our society.

It can show someone devoted to religion or someone trying to escape any organized institution involving powerful authority.

STRAIGHT

This card represents spiritual teaching, following a doctrine, and conformism. The person who gets this card might be following a traditional lifestyle or engaging in a strict behavior as the result of the education they've received. You practice orthodox values and a conventional way of living.

IN A READING ABOUT LOVE: You are attracted to traditional people and you choose them based on your beliefs and tradition, avoiding those who might be considered "taboo." Sometimes it can indicate marriage or a relationship between two people with the same ideals and beliefs.

IN A READING ABOUT CAREER: You want to play the game safely, respecting all the rules and finding connection to your group of colleagues. It can also indicate the presence of a mentor or the need to learn more.

IN A READING ABOUT MONEY: You should keep your money safe in traditional institutions. Don't engage in new ways of making money. It can also suggest that you pay more attention to the spiritual world than the material one.

REVERSED

You're feeling oppressed by an excess of rules and restrictions. You don't feel like you should follow your old beliefs or traditions, as they no longer reflect who you are. Perhaps your faith is on standby and you need to explore a new way to approach it. You want to be in control of your life without depending on orthodox ways of living.

IN A READING ABOUT LOVE: You might have lost the excitement in your current relationship or either you or they might be too judgmental. Do not follow all the advice you receive and instead focus on those who care about you.

IN A READING ABOUT CAREER: You might feel restricted by too many rules and tired of following orders given by other people. Consider if it's best to surrender for a short period of time in order to fix your problems or change jobs.

IN A READING ABOUT MONEY: You might act arrogantly about your financial state, and perhaps you feel confident enough to start a new project. However, think carefully about the risks you're willing to take.

THE LOVERS: 6

STRAIGHT: The union of opposites, partnership

REVERSED: Disharmony, imbalance

ELEMENT: Air

ASTROLOGY: Gemini

When we look at some representations of the Lovers in the Marseilles Deck, we can see three people. There is a teenage boy who has found himself between two young girls, and he has to pick one. One girl is "pleasure" and the other "virtue"; above them, Cupid is ready to shoot the arrow. In this scenario, it may be an unromantic love.

THE LOVERS

In the Rider-Waite-Smith deck, the whole picture and message are completely changed: We see two adults, mature figures, depicted in the garden of Eden. And what is even more interesting is that here, Adam and Eve—one near the tree of life and the other near the tree of knowledge—are not condemned, but are blessed by the Archangel Raphael. Raphael, the angel of air, associated with Gemini, symbolizes communication, which is the foundation of a healthy relationship.

This card is almost a blessing, a sign of harmony and balance not only between two people but two opposite forces, the masculine and feminine energies.

STRAIGHT

When the Lovers are upright it shows cohesion, the union between people (not necessarily a romantic union). It can indicate the moment where we have to make a choice between two opposites. It might also signal a harmonious romantic relationship, or it can be related to you on a personal level. It might be time for you to decide what you truly believe and love. It is (arguably) a consequence of what the Hierophant has taught us, and that's why it's the right moment to follow our own philosophy.

IN A READING ABOUT LOVE: This is a good card for love matters. It shows two people who love and care for each other with mutual respect. Sometimes it might predict a hard decision that must be made in order to welcome or maintain a romantic relationship.

IN A READING ABOUT CAREER: There is a harmonious and productive atmosphere at your workplace. You might soon be in a situation where you will make important decisions that will affect your career. This can also reveal a platonic love that has the potential to blossom.

IN A READING ABOUT MONEY: There are important decisions to be made, and you will have to pick between two options to guarantee your financial stability. It can also predict a marriage connected to wealth.

REVERSED

You are feeling discontent and disconnected from yourself or your lover. You're experiencing conflicts that could affect what you're passionate about. There can be major problems with communicating with a partner or potential lover and aligning your beliefs with your life. This card reversed might also show a refusal to take responsibility.

IN A READING ABOUT LOVE: It can indicate you're struggling to communicate and bring balance into your relationship. There is a need to resolve the issues and strengthen the bond. If you're single you might be involved in an active dating situation. However, stay true to your beliefs and ask yourself if you're being honest about your desires.

IN A READING ABOUT CAREER: A lack of teamwork and communication might cause problems in your workplace. You might be forcing a partnership or perhaps someone is not doing the work and is slowing everyone down.

IN A READING ABOUT MONEY: A project or source of additional money will not give you the desired results. Your choices could be too irrational and this could threaten your financial situation.

THE CHARIOT: 7

STRAIGHT: Willpower, travel

REVERSED: Lack of ambition, aggression

ELEMENT: Water

ASTROLOGY: Cancer

The Chariot depicts a man who is leaving a town behind, a symbol of his past. The man is ready to start a new adventure and he represents strength and determination.

THE CHARIOT

There are many esoteric symbols in this card. Let's start with the two moons on the man's shoulders, one crescent and the other waxing, under a starry canopy; this represents the spiritual influence that is guiding him.

The crown is a sign of virtue and the square on his chest represents the element Earth and grounded actions. He's holding a scepter with a golden point, which is connected with his pure and noble values and objectives. The sun with wings is the symbol of the solar hero as well as Isis, the goddess of magick arts.

The two most prominent symbols are the two sphinxes, one black and one white, representing two opposing forces going in opposite directions. It almost seems like they're trying to stop the vehicle from moving. This is because the charioteer must learn to control them—only his willpower will generate movement.

The black sphinx will cause too much emotivity, while the white one will cause too much rationality; however, they're both wearing black and white headgear, symbols of a compromise between the two. The man needs balance, the will to succeed, and the ability to tame the duality of the sphinxes.

STRAIGHT

The Chariot upright indicates a need to take control over a situation and resolve conflicts with ourselves or other people. You need to take a strong stance to reach your goals; it requires willpower, focus, tenacity, and determination. You might explore a side of yourself that you weren't aware of; that will be the result of your persistence in self-exploration.

IN A READING ABOUT LOVE: This is the time to focus on yourself—learn what you want and take time to understand what you need. If you're in a relationship, it is time to take control of your feelings. This will bring more harmony between you and your partner.

IN A READING ABOUT CAREER: This card signals that you have all the necessary potential to reach your goals. Keep your destination clear in your mind—with confidence and determination, you will get there. It is important to stay away from distractions.

IN A READING ABOUT MONEY: You might feel the need to speed things up in matters related to your money. However, you should stay focused and take your time to resolve any issue.

REVERSED

There is a lack of control that leads to feeling overwhelmed, with a high level of stress. Things are slipping out of hand and you're struggling to keep up with events. This is a great chance to be more aware of your lack of willpower and focus on learning how to listen more to your inner guidance.

IN A READING ABOUT LOVE: Tensions and disagreements are making your relationship imbalanced. If you're looking for love, patience is the key. Stay focused and love will find you. This card can also mean that you're interested in two different people.

IN A READING ABOUT CAREER: You might have to make a decision, and feel confused about what to do. A feud with colleagues or too much information at once could make you feel overwhelmed. Do not live passively and try to grow your ambitions.

IN A READING ABOUT MONEY: You might be too quick to spend your money, or perhaps you want to rush a decision that could potentially make you more money. A lack of knowledge might cause you to make the wrong decisions.

STRENGTH: 8

STRAIGHT: Compassion, inner power

REVERSED: Insecurity, jealousy

ELEMENT: Fire

ASTROLOGY: Leo

On this card we can see a woman resting atop a lion. We can feel a sense of peace and tranquility—she's not scared of the lion. There's a loving and calming expression on her face. Her ability to dominate the lion doesn't come from physical strength but quite the opposite—inner strength.

THE STRENGTH

We don't see many symbols in this card. The sky takes up a lot of space. The lion represents desire and passion, but also anger and jealousy. All fears and adversities must be faced. What really counts is believing in ourselves and having the inner strength necessary to go through life with courage and compassion.

In some decks, this card has the number 11, or it may even be depicted with other animals or the name "Lust," which changes the message completely. However, here the number eight is present as the sign of infinity above the woman's head; this is Leo's number and we can also find it in the Magician's card. This is because it's the extension of that same infinite energy, the esoteric feminine energy that is at the base of the universe.

STRAIGHT

You have the ability to stay calm and focused during stressful times; your inner strength is substantial and your heart is filled with compassion for others. You have been through challenges in life and they taught you how to navigate hard times while maintaining courage and kindness. Your stability and honesty will pay off, leading you to accomplish your goals.

IN A READING ABOUT LOVE: You could be in a very passionate relationship which could lead to a stable connection or bring anger and jealousy. It's empathy and calmness that will resolve your problems or help you find a loving partner.

IN A READING ABOUT CAREER: Listen to your rational side and your intuitive one; you know how to get through challenges, and this skill will lead you to great results if you keep going. If you would like to start a new project or career, this is your time to do it.

IN A READING ABOUT MONEY: Your ability to manage your finances has given you stability; this is a chance to make an important decision if you need to and allow yourself to spend more money than usual.

REVERSED

This card reversed indicates that you're experiencing high levels of anger and engaging in overly instinctive actions. Your inner and outer selves are in conflict, and you have lost track of what joy and happiness are. It is advised that you stop following your ego and regain your confidence.

IN A READING ABOUT LOVE: The fear of expressing your feelings—as well as the barrier you've built around yourself—won't lead you to love or true happiness. Empathy and understanding are the keys if you're in a relationship or if you're looking for one.

IN A READING ABOUT CAREER: Aggressiveness might lead to failure and make you feel like you're unable to achieve your dreams. Stop second-guessing yourself—boosting your confidence will eventually help you feel fulfilled.

IN A READING ABOUT MONEY: This could suggest you're spending your money on things you don't need or that you don't want to spend money on necessary things. The issue that needs to be solved is your sense of instability regarding your finances.

THE HERMIT: 9

STRAIGHT: Solitude, inner guidance

REVERSED: Loneliness, isolation

ELEMENT: Earth

ASTROLOGY: Virgo

The Hermit is an old man standing at the peak of a mountain, holding a lantern and a stick. The mountain represents arrival at the destination—accomplishment. Inside the lantern, we can see a star, the Seal of Solomon, a sign of wisdom. The stick is the symbol of authority.

THE HERMIT

The Hermit is going through the same mountainous path as the Fool. While the Fool is following his inner child, the Hermit is aware of where he is going and ready to share his wisdom with others. The path that he walked made him comfortable with solitude. He chose to stay away from distractions to discover his real self.

This card might scare those who are afraid of being alone, embracing the silence, and embarking on a journey where we discover ourselves.

STRAIGHT

You are ready to follow spiritual guidance that will lead you on a journey to know yourself better. You are balanced, introspective, and have good self-esteem. You might be following the guide that is within or a guru; either way, it is your time to stay away from the crowd, people's opinions, and distractions. Welcome solitude into your life. Take this time to align with yourself and strengthen your inner balance.

IN A READING ABOUT LOVE: You might need some time on your own to think about what you really want outside of the relationship, and to regain your independence. Talk to your partner about it—it might be difficult but the outcome will be positive.

IN A READING ABOUT CAREER: You might lack peace at your workplace, needing more solitude and fulfillment. Think about what you'd like to achieve. Perhaps it is time to go your own way by starting something yourself.

IN A READING ABOUT MONEY: You're realizing that money is not everything and that you need to be more grounded in spirituality. This card can also mean you need to seek advice on managing your finances.

REVERSED

You might need more time on your own. Do not refuse guidance and wisdom and do not be scared of solitude. This card reversed can also indicate that you're too involved in staying on your own, digging into your subconscious. This can be harmful at times, as what you can see from within might not always be pleasant. The best thing to do is to find a balance between introspection and sharing your time with other people.

IN A READING ABOUT LOVE: If you are in a relationship, you might feel disconnected from your partner. Self-awareness and introspection can help you find the solution to build a stronger connection. If you're single, take this time alone to understand your needs and goals before starting a new relationship.

IN A READING ABOUT CAREER: This can mean you're being forced to work on your own and your alone time might be extended further; on the other hand, it can mean you're ready to build new connections, to end your time of contemplation and be part of society again.

IN A READING ABOUT MONEY: It is time to be open to external advice on how to improve your financial situation. Do not avoid facing issues and listen to those who are wiser than you.

WHEEL OF FORTUNE: 10

STRAIGHT: Good luck, change

REVERSED: Lack of control, bad luck

ELEMENT: Fire

ASTROLOGY: Jupiter

On this card, there isn't a character but rather an object, a wheel, surrounded by many esoteric symbols. The four figures in each corner, following the definition of the prophet Ezekiel, are representative of the four zodiac signs, connected to the four cardinal points and seasons.

WHEEL OF FORTUNE

The first figure, in the top left, is an angelic symbol of the zodiac sign Aquarius. The second one, going clockwise, is the eagle, a symbol of Scorpio. The third figure is a lion, representing the sign of Leo. The last one is a bull, the symbol of Taurus. The Wheel marks the changing of the seasons.

These four representations are also connected to the Minor Arcana, respectively:

ANGEL: air, swords

EAGLE: water, cups

LION: fire, wands

BULL: earth, pentacles

The Wheel is our destiny, the karmic cycle of reincarnation represented by the snake that is descending to Anubi, the underworld. On top of the wheel, we find the sphinx, who reminds us that anything that dies is then reborn, that every action has a reaction, and that everything is always changing.

The penultimate symbol is the writing inside the wheel, which can be read in both directions: TARO is the tarots while ORAT—from the Latin word meaning "to talk"—reminds us that words help effect change. The last symbol is the Hebraic word inside the wheel, which forms the name of God. Each symbol corresponds to the signs of the Minor Arcana.

STRAIGHT

Don't resist changes, whether they're good or bad. Even if you don't understand the reason for certain events, everything will eventually make sense and turn into something positive. Always remember that everything is constantly changing.

IN A READING ABOUT LOVE: Good changes are coming. You could improve your current relationship or find a new love that will make you happy. Remember that the Wheel is always turning.

IN A READING ABOUT CAREER: It is a good time to make big changes and to look for new opportunities. Even if it might be hard, you will obtain positive results.

IN A READING ABOUT MONEY: Get ready to face big changes. Make sure to guarantee your financial stability and keep an eye out for good opportunities.

REVERSED

You're avoiding making big changes and facing reality because you're too scared of the outcome. Although luck has not been on your side, to get rid of this feeling of inactivity you must learn to release what no longer serves you.

IN A READING ABOUT LOVE: Expect misunderstanding and temporary problems between you and your partner. Communication and patience will eventually get you out of this situation.

IN A READING ABOUT CAREER: It is not the right time to make changes. Be aware of your lack of commitment, find your balance, and let go of past expectations.

IN A READING ABOUT MONEY: You will experience issues and instability regarding your money. Make sure to have some savings and avoid big investments.

JUSTICE: 11

STRAIGHT: Cause and effect, legal matters

REVERSED: Unfairness, dishonesty

ELEMENT: Air

ASTROLOGY: Libra

Justice is represented by the Greek goddess Themis. She's holding a sword and a scale. The sword is a symbol of air and the mind, while the scale shows how intuition is balanced with logic. It is clear that her choices are decisive and unchangeable.

JUSTICE

She will assure order. She's looking straight forward, so we can see that no one can escape her. The two columns ensure her firmness and fairness in the decisions she makes.

STRAIGHT

Justice tells you that all your actions have long-term consequences and that there will always come a time when you'll see the results of your past decisions. This card changes meaning depending on your situation. If you caused pain to someone you'll soon have to face the consequences. Alternatively, it can encourage you to seek truth in others' actions. It can also mean you need to pay attention to a specific aspect of your life and resolve any insecurities.

IN A READING ABOUT LOVE: Karma is at the base of this card. If you've been giving love and kindness, you will receive them. If you've acted negatively or aggressively, be ready to face the consequences. It is always the right time to improve your behavior and actions.

IN A READING ABOUT CAREER: Always make professional decisions based on fairness and integrity. A positive mindset and actions will pay you back with good results and deals.

IN A READING ABOUT MONEY: Keep balance and fairness in mind when dealing with money. Do not be selfish or follow bad patterns and your finances will be fine.

REVERSED

Justice reversed could mean unfairness in a legal decision or that you're being treated unfairly. It can also mean you're refusing to face the consequences of your actions. There's always time to change course and make things better.

IN A READING ABOUT LOVE: There's an imbalance between you and your partner, and compromises might be made. If you're single it is time to rethink your expectations and keep being patient without blaming others.

IN A READING ABOUT CAREER: You could face legal problems connected to your work or an imbalance between colleagues. If you've lied to someone or you're witnessing unfairness, always remember to act morally.

IN A READING ABOUT MONEY: There's dishonesty connected to your money. Someone is lying to you or you don't want to admit your mistakes. It is not a good time to make plans to find additional income.

THE HANGED MAN: 12

STRAIGHT: Sacrifice, seeing things from
another perspective

REVERSED: Stagnation, useless sacrifices

ELEMENT: Water

ASTROLOGY: Neptune

On this card, we can see a
man hanging by only one
of his feet from a living
tree. From his face, we can
see he's peaceful. The light
around his head makes it
clear that he's in a positive
state of being.

THE HANGED MAN

He chose to be there in
that position, and we can
assume this by looking at
the positions of his feet and arms. The hanging
position is a symbol of attachment to the light and
spiritual value.

The man in the card doesn't care about the opinions that others might have of him. He chooses to
see the world from his perspective without being
influenced by others.

The yellow of his shoes, clothes, and light is a symbol of his intellect.

STRAIGHT

A moment of calm—and perhaps certain sacrifices—is needed to obtain the results you want. You know you need this time to stay on your own and think about your next move. Your vision of life and the world is different compared to those of your peers, but despite that, it will lead you to accomplishment. This card can also indicate it's time to put certain actions on pause. This may bring indecision, but it is necessary.

IN A READING ABOUT LOVE: You might be trying to rush finding a new love but the key is waiting for the right time. If you're in a relationship, your commitment could be tested, and it is time to decide if you want to stay or leave.

IN A READING ABOUT CAREER: Changes need to be made and you're aware of it. However, you should not rush it—take all the time you need. Look at things from your perspective and make the right decision.

IN A READING ABOUT MONEY: You might have experienced stress because of your finances. You can turn negatives into positives if you try to look at things from a new perspective and let go of old attachments.

REVERSED

You are at the mercy of events, making decisions more to please others than yourself. Work on not making all your decisions because you're scared of what people could think of you. Sacrificing time only for others could lead to unfulfillment.

IN A READING ABOUT LOVE: Do not sacrifice your time for someone who is not as involved as you are. This is your time to take action, understand what you want, and make changes.

IN A READING ABOUT CAREER: You feel stuck and powerless, like you're not getting any results. This could be because of your fear to change paths. Perhaps you could consider being more active in working toward your future.

IN A READING ABOUT MONEY: Letting go of your past and old attachments could help you avoid a big loss. Learn from your past mistakes—this way you will stop losing money.

DEATH: 13

STRAIGHT: Transformation, changes

REVERSED: Refusal to change, stagnation

ELEMENT: Water

ASTROLOGY: Scorpio

Death is depicted by a living skeleton riding a white horse. His armor shows his invincibility—that no one can win over death. The rose on the flag represents purity and the power that death has. The white horse shows that death purifies everyone.

DEATH

Beneath the horse we see people of different ages and classes, as death does not care about your background. Death is going toward the east, where the sun is reborn, while the others look toward the west, where the sun dies.

STRAIGHT

Although the name of the card often scares those who see it, its meaning is not as dark as one may think. This card marks the end of a chapter, a door that is closing, and reveals a new start. You must learn how important it is to move forward, leave the past in the past, and be open to new things coming your way.

IN A READING ABOUT LOVE: There are patterns that are damaging your relationship. You and your partner need to find a new way to communicate and interact with each other. This could also mean the end of a difficult relationship.

IN A READING ABOUT CAREER: You're attached to your stability, even if it has caused dissatisfaction and unhappiness. The course of events could force you to make some changes.

IN A READING ABOUT MONEY: You're not in a prosperous time. However, the mistakes you made will be a lesson and help you turn the situation around.

REVERSED

You are resistant to changes; you're too scared to welcome new beginnings and this makes you stagnant. Life, however, goes on, and you should come to terms with impermanence. Making positive changes is one way to love ourselves.

IN A READING ABOUT LOVE: You're hanging on to a relationship that is no longer meant to be. This is leading you to unhealthy behaviors. If you're single, you need to let go of negative thoughts and patterns before you welcome a new love.

IN A READING ABOUT CAREER: There could be self-sabotaging and unhealthy life choices. You could be struggling to quit a job that is making you unhappy. Sometimes changes are essential.

IN A READING ABOUT MONEY: Too much spending or bad financial choices are making your finances unsustainable. You don't want to let go of these habits because you're too scared of change.

TEMPERANCE: 14

STRAIGHT: Moderation, patience

REVERSED: Excess, imbalance

ELEMENT: Fire

ASTROLOGY: Sagittarius

There are two interpretations regarding who the subject of this card is. It might be the Archangel Michael, who empties a cup from which no one will drink. It is a symbol of abstinence and can also predict an illness. It can be seen as the card that indicates temptation (as the card following

TEMPERANCE

this one is the Devil), suggesting that we should not surrender to evil habits.

Another interpretation is that the angel is androgynous. There's a balance between the genders, with one foot in the water, representing the subconscious, and the other touching earth, which represents the material world.

The two cups symbolize the conscious and subconscious mind while the water symbolizes union.

The square and the triangle symbolizes the union between Earth and the holy trinity. The radiant sun on the angel's forehead represents growth in awareness.

This card shows moderation and balance between opposites.

STRAIGHT

You're an extremely calm and balanced person. Your mindset and personality protect you from external problems and anxiety. You're patient and you know exactly where you're going and what you want, and this is no small feat. This card can also suggest staying away from temptations and balancing your inner and outer selves.

IN A READING ABOUT LOVE: Let your relationship evolve without too much ego. You might engage in excessive behaviors, so remember to stay calm and balanced.

IN A READING ABOUT CAREER: Your workplace will be harmonious and cooperative. Remember to balance work and private life. Your efforts will pay off.

IN A READING ABOUT MONEY: Income might be slow but your moderation made your finances stable. Don't hesitate to spend some money on yourself.

REVERSED

This can indicate a lack of control and also addiction to alcohol or drugs. There's a major imbalance in your life that could also be the result of a lack of planning.

IN A READING ABOUT LOVE: Trying to rush a situation or letting extreme emotions take over could cause problems in your relationship. You could also be too demanding of the person you're dating.

IN A READING ABOUT CAREER: You're struggling to find the balance between work and personal life. There's a lack of cooperation and effort in your work.

IN A READING ABOUT MONEY: A lack of confidence stops you from enjoying your money.

THE DEVIL: 15

STRAIGHT: Materialism, indulgence

REVERSED: Release, self-improvement

ELEMENT: Earth

ASTROLOGY: Capricorn

The Devil in this card is Baphomet, one of the most popular representations of this figure. The raised hand, with the fingers separated in the middle, testifies to the importance of materialism in our world, while the torch he holds lights something dark and impure. His face, similar to his zodiac sign,

THE DEVIL

Capricorn, has two horns—a symbol of instinct.

The bat wings are a sign of the absence of spirituality; everything is material and part of the mundane world. The man and the woman remind us of a dark version of the Lovers, as they made the wrong choice and are now servants of this card, as is represented by the chains that bind them. Their tails, made of grapes and fire, are symbols of their addiction to power and pleasure.

This card reveals passion, addiction to dark pleasures, and the material world.

STRAIGHT

You're dependent on material things. You find pleasure in situations that will cause you unhappiness in the long term. You are a slave to this kind of pleasure and although you're aware of it, you don't want to get yourself out of this situation.

IN A READING ABOUT LOVE: There's a need to follow the path of self-pleasure to satisfy your desires. This can lead to selfish behaviors or addiction to a relationship. While there's nothing wrong with having fun, make sure you're not hurting others.

IN A READING ABOUT CAREER: You might be stuck in a job you don't like and unaware of the imbalance between professional and private life. Instead of blaming others, find the solution within yourself—you have the power to change.

IN A READING ABOUT MONEY: You should ask yourself if you're too attracted to money and the material world and if this is affecting your behavior. Changing the way you handle your finances could be the solution.

REVERSED

You're stuck in a position you feel you have no control over. While it might be easier to blame others or bad luck, it is time to do some inner work and fight your addictions. Avoid quick solutions and try to see things from a different angle.

IN A READING ABOUT LOVE: It is time to leave an unhealthy relationship or work on toxic behaviors. You have the power to set yourself free from these difficult aspects of your life and regain happiness.

IN A READING ABOUT CAREER: Plan the changes you want to make in your career and take action. This can mean leaving your job or improving the situation in your workplace.

IN A READING ABOUT MONEY: You're working on past mistakes and trying to improve your financial situation. Keep working on it and you'll finally find some stability.

THE TOWER: 16

STRAIGHT: Major changes, disaster

REVERSED: Avoiding suffering, fear of changes

ELEMENT: Fire

ASTROLOGY: Mars

The Tower is a difficult card, as its meaning is strong and hard to face. We can see a tower struck by lightning, making the roof (the crown) fall down. Something difficult will suddenly happen and this suggests that we run away to escape it.

With the Devil, we've seen unhealthy patterns,

THE TOWER

and now they are brought to light and we must get rid of negative energies. The drops of fire are the representation of the Yod, one of the four letters of the Tetragrammaton (the name of God in the Hebrew Bible); the fire will lead us to take new actions. There are 10 drops of fire on the left and 12 on the right; the 10 are the planets, the 12 are the zodiac signs, and the sum is 22, the number of the Major Arcana. From this card, we can see that something painful must end to give space to something new.

STRAIGHT

You've been ignoring some issues in your life and now you're paying the price. Something difficult will happen and open your eyes. Although it doesn't mean that something terrible is going to happen, a radical change is needed.

IN A READING ABOUT LOVE: Some major changes are needed in your relationship or perhaps it is time for a breakup. Take your time to think deeply about what you want from love and make all the necessary changes.

IN A READING ABOUT CAREER: Something will happen in your workplace. It could be the arrival of a new boss, new colleagues, or a sudden stressful environment. Consider if this is the time to change jobs and focus on your stability.

IN A READING ABOUT MONEY: There might be unpleasant surprises, such as unexpected losses or issues that will slow down your income. Make sure to have some savings.

REVERSED

You're resisting changes that deep down you know must be made. You haven't learned from negative experiences and that's why you're not fully facing reality. However, changes will happen no matter what—when you will welcome them you will also enjoy freedom.

IN A READING ABOUT LOVE: You're ignoring some important signs that there's something wrong in your relationship. The more you ignore these problems, the bigger they will get.

IN A READING ABOUT CAREER: You're going through a stressful time, and although you might think it is a positive thing, it doesn't mean you will feel fulfilled after. Maybe it's time to look elsewhere.

IN A READING ABOUT MONEY: You're trying to keep everything together to avoid disaster. However, sometimes it is better to surrender to be free from any preoccupations.

THE STAR: 17

STRAIGHT: Hope, good fortune

REVERSED: Discouragement, lack of faith

ELEMENT: Air

ASTROLOGY: Aquarius

The Star shows a woman at the edge of a small pond, pouring water from two amphorae, one onto the ground, the other into the pond. This is nurturing the nature around her, and we can see a flourishing field in this harmonious environment.

THE STAR

One foot is in water, a symbol of her spiritual abilities, and the other, touching the ground, is a symbol of strength. The bird on the tree is the holy ibis of thought.

The seven stars, however, have many different interpretations. There are those who believe they are the seven chakras, and others say it's a way of representing the seven planets of ancient astronomy, the Pleiades, or Seven Sisters.

A card rich in emotions, it brings peace and harmony and invites us to take a break in order to find our true path.

STRAIGHT

The time of struggles and problems is now over. You can take a breath and enjoy the peace that surrounds you. It is the moment of a new, positive start, where you have clear objectives and dreams. Have faith in the universe and never lose your courage to act.

IN A READING ABOUT LOVE: Your positivity will attract only good energies and people. If you've been struggling in your relationship, you will experience a great understanding with your partner. Keep being honest and everything will turn out well.

IN A READING ABOUT CAREER: This is the perfect time to set goals and work toward your dreams. Take this time not only to work professionally but also to work on your inner peace.

IN A READING ABOUT MONEY: Your positive mindset will help you improve your financial situation and enjoy the results. Always be grateful for what you have and what you will obtain in the future.

REVERSED

You might feel uninspired or disconnected from yourself; you feel like it is not your time to shine and this is bringing your mood down. You've lost faith in something and this is causing negative thoughts. This card reversed is a reminder to keep hope alive.

IN A READING ABOUT LOVE: Your sense of being unworthy of love and your lack of confidence have repercussions, affecting not only your feelings but also how others perceive you. Don't be too hard on yourself and learn to appreciate who you are.

IN A READING ABOUT CAREER: Your lack of faith and creativity is affecting the way you work. Although the situation could appear negative to you, you should consider seeing things from a different angle and try to be more positive.

IN A READING ABOUT MONEY: Your finances might not have been doing very well recently, but your lack of faith is also affecting this. Remember you still have hope that you can sort everything out.

THE MOON: 18

STRAIGHT: Intuition, illusions

REVERSED: Fear, doubts

ELEMENT: Water

ASTROLOGY: Pisces

The Moon is a card full of deep messages and partic-ular symbols. Within the Moon itself, we can see the profile of a human face. The expression shows us it's con-centrating, contemplating with a veil of mystery.

THE MOON

Its enormous power is dripping down to where a dog and a wolf are trying to absorb it. The two animals are the symbol of our animalistic nature; the dog is civilized while the wolf is wild and indomitable.

Beneath them a crustacean is emerging from the water. It never stops, putting itself in others' path, trying to slow them down, reminding them to always pay attention.

The two towers are good and evil and they reveal how difficult it can be to differentiate between them

in life. This is because we must go beyond appearances to understand the true identity of a person or
the real nature of a situation. The only way to do so
is to let the moonlight inspire our inner guidance
and unconscious mind.

STRAIGHT

You're connected to your intuition, creativity, inner
voice, and everything that involves the lunar energies. Your inner mind is the light that will guide
you through uncertain times. Pay attention to
signs, dreams, and feelings—they might be the
answer you were looking for. Always be aware of
possible illusions and hidden truths.

IN A READING ABOUT LOVE: You could be
in a highly emotional relationship that is causing
stress and anxiety. Dig into your subconscious
to understand what could be holding you back
from accepting love.

IN A READING ABOUT CAREER: Your
workplace might be full of tensions or perhaps
your goals are unclear. There is a dark side that
you're not aware of; it is not necessarily negative,
but it is a sign that you need to go beyond illusions and doubts.

IN A READING ABOUT MONEY: It is not
the right time to make financial decisions. Ask

questions and ensure you are certain of the solutions. You could experience ups and downs before finding clarity.

REVERSED

You are on the dark side of the Moon, experiencing doubts, anxiety, and confusion. It is time to listen to your inner voice, dig deeper into your intuition, and use this time to reflect. This can also mean you're slowly getting rid of these emotions and getting closer to the light. Another meaning in this card reversed is the need to resolve past issues with a female figure; that could be your mom or another woman in your life.

IN A READING ABOUT LOVE: Be aware of possible manipulation, confusion, and deception. Not everything is as it seems. You might not be always honest with your partner, or you will soon notice some lies.

IN A READING ABOUT CAREER: Your anxiety and uncertainty are turning your work experience into a stressful and difficult one. The communication level is very low and paranoia could worsen everything. On the other hand, you could be finally going beyond your fears and doubts and finding some balance.

IN A READING ABOUT MONEY: You could be finding the light you needed to improve your finances or, alternatively, doubts and fear could make everything worse. Listen to your intuition before making any decision.

THE SUN: 19

STRAIGHT: Success, happiness

REVERSED: Overconfidence, negativity

ELEMENT: Fire

ASTROLOGY: Sun

With the Moon we were in the dark, risking encountering illusions, but with the Sun we can welcome light and warmth. Everything about this card represents joy, life, and energy.

The Sun is what gives us life and optimism; the naked child represents innocence and alignment

THE SUN

with ourselves. The white horse is another sign of

purity, but also of strength and nobility. The child has nothing to hide, giving us clarity, stability, and a clear mind.

STRAIGHT

This is your time to shine. This card predicts success, abundance, fulfilment, and joy. You're in charge of your life right now; you know where you're going and you're ready to welcome good results. You have the skills to help and inspire others, providing love and stability to those around you.

IN A READING ABOUT LOVE: You're in a happy relationship full of love and respect. You're building a strong connection based on harmony and kindness. If you're looking for love, it is the perfect time to find romance.

IN A READING ABOUT CAREER: You will finally receive the recognition you deserve. It is a moment for abundance, fulfilment, and celebration.

IN A READING ABOUT MONEY: Your finances are stable and you are enjoying abundance and happiness. If there were unresolved issues, they will all be resolved.

REVERSED

When we get this card reversed, it doesn't necessarily

mean something negative is going to happen. It could indicate things are going slowly or that we feel unworthy of happiness and love. It can also indicate that you're being unrealistic about a specific aspect of your life. A moment of introspection to think about what is blocking you from enjoying progress is needed.

IN A READING ABOUT LOVE: You could be taking your partner for granted or perhaps feeling bored and unmotivated. Your ego or superficial things such as money could make you feel disconnected. Take time to appreciate what you have and let the sun shine.

IN A READING ABOUT CAREER: Everything that the sun brings is positive but now there are some clouds covering your abilities. You could be feeling overwhelmed, depressed, and burned out. Ask yourself if maybe you had unrealistic expectations.

IN A READING ABOUT MONEY: You could be feeling too confident in your actions and this could lead you to arrogance. Lower your expectations and try to resolve any issue with logic rather than ego.

JUDGMENT: 20

STRAIGHT: Reflection, choices

REVERSED: Avoiding changes, unawareness

ELEMENT: Fire

ASTROLOGY: Pluto

On this card, we can see the Archangel Gabriel playing his trumpet. We can see men, women, and children rising from their graves, ready, with open arms, to receive the last judgment.

The large mountains in the background remind us that judgment is inevitable and no one can escape from

JUDGMENT

it. Although this can seem like a strictly "Catholic" message, it is important to remark that tarot has no religion.

When the first recorded tarot decks were created in the Middle Ages, the Catholic church was going through dark times. Despite that, tarot still adopted some images from Catholicism and other mono-theistic religions as a way to send us general and universal messages.

This card is the symbol of something new coming, a call to compare who we were and who we are now, and a reminder to take a moment of self-reflection.

STRAIGHT

This card indicates self-awareness and a need for reflection. You'll have to deal with the repercussions of past actions, which will lead you to close an old chapter. This is the time to face our past and never look back afterward.

IN A READING ABOUT LOVE: Resolve any issue you've been avoiding and always be open with your partner about what needs to change. Whether you did good or bad things in the past, now is the time to face the consequences.

IN A READING ABOUT CAREER: Maybe you're thinking of changing jobs and finding one that more closely reflects who you are. Make all the changes that are necessary and always take responsibility for your actions.

IN A READING ABOUT MONEY: Take this time to think about your relationship with money. Release all unhealthy behaviors and practice more maturity in managing your finances.

REVERSED

You're having a hard time confronting yourself and admitting to your mistakes, fears, and bad decisions. Avoiding changes is never a good pattern to follow, especially when they are necessary. You might be doubting and judging yourself too much; use your past mistakes as tools for improvement.

IN A READING ABOUT LOVE: Your partner or you could be too judgmental and unwilling to compromise. Take this time to openly work on healthy changes.

IN A READING ABOUT CAREER: You are being too hard on yourself, not letting your mistakes go. If the job you're doing now doesn't fulfill you, maybe it's time to think about what changes you can make. This card can also indicate a refusal to take responsibility.

IN A READING ABOUT MONEY: There are things that are holding you back from improving your finances. Following the same patterns won't help you solve the issues. Be open to changes and don't beat yourself up.

THE WORLD: 21

STRAIGHT: Wholeness, fulfilment

REVERSED: Discontent, incompletion

ELEMENT: Earth

ASTROLOGY: Saturn

We are now at the end of the journey that started with the Fool. We've been through all the elements and paths we encounter in life and we are concluding it with the World.

THE WORLD

In the center of the card, there's a dancing woman holding two wands, a sign of constant movement and evolution. The big laurel crown is an ancient symbol of victory, while the ribbons are a symbol of infinity.

The four figures on the corners are the same we found on the Wheel of Fortune: the angel, the eagle, the lion, and the bull. They symbolize the four evangelists, the four cardinal zodiac signs (Aquarius, Scorpio, Leo, and Taurus), and the four elements. Together they reveal the harmony of all forces and energies.

This is a highly harmonious and peaceful card that signals achievement and the joyful completion of a journey.

STRAIGHT

You're encountering great success and results in whatever field of life you're focusing on—that could be love, money, career, or family. There's a sense of wholeness and certainty in your ability to achieve all your goals. After big challenges and all the experiences you have had in life, now it's time for completion, to welcome the good results from all your hard work. All your accomplishments are free of selfishness, as you learned how to share and care for those around you.

IN A READING ABOUT LOVE: Your relationship is mature, based on love and respect. You are planning your future with your loved one and everything will go accordingly. If you're single, you learned how to be happy on your own first and you're now ready to start a stable relationship.

IN A READING ABOUT CAREER: Enjoy all the rewards that you're receiving. You will be able to finish all your projects and see the results of your commitment and effort.

IN A READING ABOUT MONEY: You are now able to resolve past issues that were affecting your finances. Your hard work is paying off and it's now time to make bigger plans.

REVERSED

You might feel confused about which road to take. You may have accomplished some goals, but they're not the ones you wanted and that's making you feel empty and unsatisfied. You're not too far from getting what you want, but you first need to resolve some issues.

IN A READING ABOUT LOVE: Some things might not have gone to plan and that's causing frustration. Something in your love life is missing and maybe you're not able to see all the positive aspects of your life. Take time to think about what you want to change.

IN A READING ABOUT CAREER: The puzzle is almost complete but you still feel some pieces are missing. What you have is not making you feel totally fulfilled. It is time to think about what your real goals are without being scared of trying to achieve them.

IN A READING ABOUT MONEY: You're not content with what you have and you risk feeling discouraged and powerless. However, stay committed to what you're doing; you're not too far from getting what you want.

CHAPTER
FOUR

TAROT
SPREADS

✦ ✳ ✦

TO HELP YOU find a clear answer to a question, you can use specific patterns known as spreads. A tarot spread is an intentional layout where each card answers a particular question. The position of each card in the spread will aid you in interpreting their meaning and thus add clarity to their message. Always remember to rely on the cards' meaning and your intuition; this is the key to a good reading!

✦ ✳ ✦

ONE CARD

This is a perfect "spread" when you need a quick and simple answer. You can also pick this spread if you want to read your tarot every day but don't have enough time to read more than one card.

PAST, PRESENT, FUTURE

This spread will help you see a general picture of the past, present, and future. You can ask a general question or pick a specific field like love, money, or work.

1 Past
2 Present
3 Future

SEVEN CARDS SPREAD

This spread will bring to light the impact of past and future events, as well as your fears or the behaviors of people around you.

1 Your current situation
2 The past
3 Past challenges
4 Lessons from the past

5 New influences
6 How they will affect you
7 The result

CELTIC CROSS

This is one of the best-known tarot spreads; it is the perfect way to gain a detailed answer to a specific question. It will give you a general view of your life and an exhaustive answer.

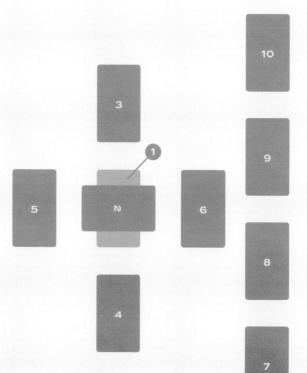

1 Your current situation
2 What is holding
you back
3 The best solution to
your current problem
4 Hidden aspects
5 The past

6 The near future
7 Your current state
of mind
8 External influences
9 Hopes or fears
10 The final result

FENG SHUI SPREAD

This spread is used by Feng Shui practitioners to discover the energies and influences affecting specific areas of your life.

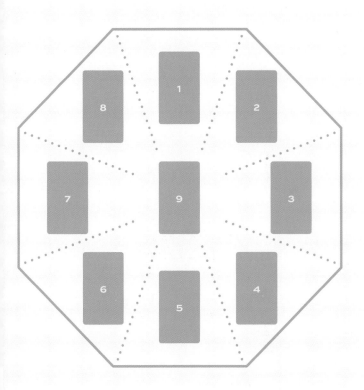

1 Fame, career, future

2 Relationships

3 Creativity

4 Friends, colleagues, travel

5 Self-identity

6 Spirituality

7 Family, community

8 Wealth

9 Health

SPREAD FOR
THE SABBATS

If you're a pagan, you're probably familiar with the sabbats. They are different festivities celebrated during the year; you can find them listed in the "Wheel of the Year" (the annual cycle of seasonal festivals observed by many pagans). This spread can be used during those days of celebration to provide more guidance.

1   What there is to learn
    during this festivity

2   Thing you have to let
    go of

3   Things that need more
    balance

4   Near future

5   Guidance until the
    next sabbat

6   Message from my
    spirit guide

RELATIONSHIP SPREAD

This spread is advised when seeking guidance regarding a specific relationship. It does not have to be romantic; it can be with a family member, a friend, or a colleague.

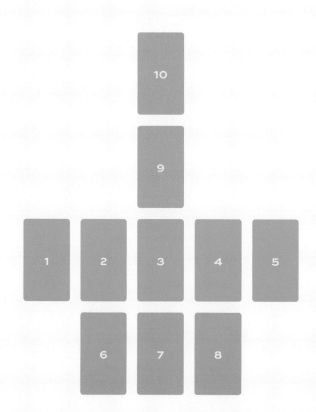

1 How the past influenced the relationship

2 Influences from the near past

3 Current situation

4 External influences

5 Future events

6 Hidden aspects

7 The path we should take

8 Future obstacles

9 Hopes or fears

10 Final outcome

SPIRAL SPREAD

This particular spread is good when we would like to understanding the development of a specific matter, taking into account how our subconscious and physical world will affect it.

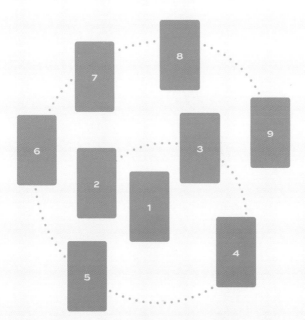

1 The essence of
  the matter

2 Past

3 Present

4 Future

5 Possibilities

6 Influences

7 Hidden aspects

8 External influences

9 Outcome

ASTROLOGICAL SPREAD

For this spread, it is not necessary to ask a specific question. Each card will represent an astrological chart, and each chart will have characteristics related to you.

1 Yourself
2 Aries (current mood)
3 Taurus (finances)
4 Gemini (communication, travel)
5 Cancer (home, family)
6 Leo (pleasure)

7 Virgo (health)
8 Libra (partner)
9 Scorpio (death, inheritance)
10 Sagittarius (spirituality, dreams)
11 Aquarius (friendship)
12 Pisces (fears)

WEEKLY SPREAD

This spread is perfect to use in anticipation of the upcoming week. The Significator here represents a general view of the week; the other cards correlate to a specific day.

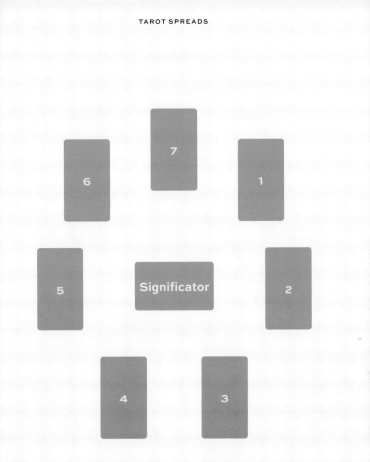

1 Monday

2 Tuesday

3 Wednesday

4 Thursday

5 Friday

6 Saturday

7 Sunday

CONCLUSION

+ ✳ +

W e're at the end of this book, and I hope with all my heart that it helped expand your knowledge about and love for tarot cards. The magickal journey is long, and the cards will never stop revealing hidden messages along the way.

The beauty of this practice is that it is infinite— we will never finish getting to know the cards, as their power to show us the way is vast and limitless. I wish for you that you are able to continuously expand your magickal abilities, guided by the power of tarot.

Remember to use this book like a friend that gives you advice; do not be scared to experiment, to discover new information, and to develop your magickal talent. The cards should not limit you. Instead, use them to find freedom and overcome any barriers.

MAY MAGICK ALWAYS BE WITH YOU. BLESSED BE!

FOUR OF WANDS

QUEEN OF CUPS

THE EMPRESS

PAGE OF PENTACLES

SEVEN OF SWORDS

ISABELLA FERRARI was born and raised in Italy. After living for more than two years at ILTK, the acclaimed Buddhist institute, she became a meditation teacher. She then lived in London for a few years to explore her interest in music and art. She is the author of *Witchcraft Simplified*, *Crystals Simplified*, and the novel *Ocean Crayon*, and wrote for her own website and many important magazines as a music journalist. Her passion for spirituality and religions inspired her to deeply study the different branches of Paganism and create her project Greenwitchcom. Find her on Instagram @greenwitchcom.

O
O O
O
DEYST.

HarperCollins books may be purchased for educational, business, or sales promotional use. For information, please email the Special Markets Department at SPsales@ harpercollins.com.

FIRST EDITION

Library of Congress Cataloging-in-Publication Data has been applied for.

ISBN 978-1-646-43371-1

23 24 25 26 27   IMG   10 9 8 7 6 5 4 3 2 1